2017

CONTEMPORARY
PLAYWRIGHTS

HAROLD PINTER
BY
RONALD HAYMAN

THIRD EDITION

H·E·B

HEINEMANN : LONDON

Heinemann Educational Books Ltd
London Edinburgh Melbourne Auckland Toronto
Singapore Hong Kong Kuala Lumpur
Nairobi Ibadan Johannesburg
Lusaka New Delhi

ISBN 0 435 18437 7 (cased edition)
ISBN 0 435 18414 8 (paperback)

Published by Heinemann Educational Books Ltd
48 Charles Street, London W1X 8AH
Printed Offset Litho and bound in Great Britain by
Cox & Wyman Ltd, London, Fakenham and Reading

CONTENTS

ACKNOWLEDGEMENTS

The Author would like to thank Catherine Barton, Martha Crewe, John Peter, Charles Tomlinson and Irving Wardle for their help in reading typescripts and making useful comments, when the series was in preparation.

The Author and Publishers wish to thank the following for permission to include quotations from the publications listed below:

Johnson over Jordan: J. B. Priestley and A. D. Peters & Co; *The Homecoming, The Collection, The Lover, Night School, A Slight Ache, The Room, The Dumb Waiter, The Birthday Party, A Night Out, The Caretaker, The Basement, Last to Go, The Dwarfs, Tea Party, Landscape, Silence, Night, Old Times*: Harold Pinter and Methuen & Co Ltd. *Monologue*: Harold Pinter and the Covent Garden Press.

The Author is grateful to the *London Magazine* for permission to incorporate part of his article 'Landscape Without Pictures' which appeared in the July 1968 issue into the chapter on *Landscape*.

The photographs of *Tea Party* and *The Basement* are reproduced by courtesy of the BBC; that of *The Homecoming* by courtesy of the Royal Court Theatre; and that of *The Caretaker* by courtesy of Michael Boys.

NOTE ON THIRD EDITION

Revisions have been made throughout the text and this edition (1974) contains new chapters on the plays *Old Times* (1971) and *Monologue* (1973) and on Pinter's writing for the cinema. The Conclusion has been revised, the Bibliography and List of Performances have been updated, and a new Biographical Outline and a Filmography have been added.

BIOGRAPHICAL OUTLINE

1930   Born in Hackney, the only child of an East End Jewish tailor.

1948   Started an interrupted training at the Royal Academy of Dramatic Art. Refused to do National Service. On trial twice as a conscientious objector.

1949   Wrote first fragment of dramatic dialogue, *Kullus*.

1950   Two poems published in *Poetry London*, August. First job as an actor – in a radio feature, *Focus on Football Pools*, September.

1951   Resumed training at Central School of Speech and Drama.

1951–52 Toured Ireland in Anew McMaster's company.

1953   Acted in Donald Wolfit's season at King's Theatre, Hammersmith. Met Vivien Merchant.

1954–57 Adopted stage name of David Barron. Worked in various repertory companies. When out of work he took jobs as a waiter, a doorman, a dishwasher and a door-to-door salesman.

1956   Met Vivien Merchant again while they were both in the repertory company at the Palace Court Theatre, Bournemouth. They were married that year.

1957   Wrote *The Room* during four afternoons while in weekly repertory at Devon, rehearsing in the mornings and playing in the evenings. Henry Woolf, who was studying at the Drama Department of Bristol University and had asked for the play, directed it there. After seeing the production, Pinter went on to write *The Dumb Waiter* and *The Birthday Party*. *The Room* was also produced by students of the Bristol Old Vic at a student drama competition sponsored by the *Sunday Times*. Harold Hobson, its drama critic, was one of the judges.

Harold Pinter

1958   On reading what Hobson wrote about the play, Michael
        Codron, an independent producer, asked to see other scripts
        by Pinter. Birth of Pinter's son, Daniel.
        Codron bought an option on *The Birthday Party* for £50.
        After one unperformed radio play, *Something in Common*, he
        wrote *A Slight Ache*, which was commissioned by the BBC.

1959   Wrote *A Night Out* and *The Caretaker*. Contributed two
        sketches 'Trouble in the Works' and 'The Black and the
        White' to the *New Lyric Revue*, presented by Codron at
        Hammersmith in July.

1960   Wrote *Night School* and the radio version of *The Dwarfs*
        based on an earlier autobiographical novel.
        Took over the part of Mick in the West End production of
        The Caretaker for four weeks from 21 February.

1961   Wrote *The Collection*.

1962   Wrote *The Lover* and screenplays for *The Caretaker* and
        The Servant (based on Robin Maugham's novella). Co-
        directed the Royal Shakespeare Company's production of
        The Collection, with Peter Hall.

1963   Wrote the screenplay for *The Pumpkin Eater* (based on
        Penelope Mortimer's novel).

1964   Wrote *Tea Party* and *The Homecoming*. Directed *The
        Birthday Party* for the Royal Shakespeare Company.

1965   Played in Philip Saville's television production of Sartre's
        Huis Clos (*No Exit*), with Jane Arden and Katherine
        Woodville. Wrote screenplay for *The Quiller Memorandum*
        (from Adam Hall's novel *The Berlin Memorandum*).

1966   Awarded a C.B.E.
        Wrote screenplay for *Accident* (based on Nicholas Mosley's
        novel) and played in it.

1967   Played Stott in television production of *The Basement*.
        Directed Robert Shaw's play *The Man in the Glass Booth*,
        with Donald Pleasence.

Biographical Outline

BIBLIOGRAPHY

Texts

The Birthday Party and Other Plays
  containing also *The Room* and *The Dumb Waiter*

A Slight Ache and Other Plays
  containing also *A Night Out, The Dwarfs* and the revue sketches

The Caretaker

The Collection and *The Lover*
  containing also a short prose piece called *The Examination*

The Homecoming

Tea Party and Other Plays
  containing also *The Basement* and *Night School*

Landscape and Silence
  containing also the sketch *Night*

  All these are published by Methuen

Mac

Landscape

  These are both published by Emanuel Wax for Pendragon Press.
  Mac is a memoir of the Irish actor-manager Anew McMaster

Old Times

Five Screenplays
  containing *The Servant, The Pumpkin Eater, The Quiller Memorandum, Accident* and *The Go-Between*

  These are both published by Methuen

Monologue

  Published in a limited edition by the Covent Garden Press

Bibliography

Poems

> Published by Enitharmon Press and distributed by Eric and
> Joad Stevens, 2 Prospect Road, London N.W.2
> Eighteen poems, including one about *The Birthday Party*,
> and a three-page fragment of dialogue, *Kullus* (1949), which
> contains the germ of the idea developed in *The Basement* (1967)

Interviews

'The Art of the Theatre' in *The Paris Review*, No. 39
> Reprinted in *Writers at Work* (Third Series), London: Secker &
> Warburg

Interview with John Russell Taylor in *Sight and Sound*
> Autumn 1966

Interview with Michael Dean, *The Listener*, 6 March 1969

Interview with Kenneth Cavander in *Behind the Scenes*, edited by
> Joseph F. McCrindle, London: Pitman.

Selected Criticism

Baker, William and Tabachnik, Stephen Ely	*Harold Pinter*, London: Oliver and Boyd
Esslin, Martin	*Pinter: A Study of His Plays*, London: Eyre Methuen
Hinchliffe, Arnold P.	*Harold Pinter*, New York: Twayne
Kerr, Walter	*Harold Pinter*, New York: Columbia Univ. Press
Lahr, John and Anthea	*A Casebook on The Homecoming*, London: Davis-Poynter
Salem, Daniel	*Harold Pinter, Dramaturge de l'ambivalence*, Paris: Denoël
Trussler, Simon	*The Plays of Harold Pinter*, London: Gollancz

Harold Pinter

Articles and Essays

Brown, John Russell   'Mr Pinter's Shakespeare' in *The Critical Quarterly*, Autumn 1963
'Dialogue in Pinter and Others' in *The Critical Quarterly*, Autumn 1965

Cohn, Ruby   'The World of Harold Pinter' in *Tulane Drama Review*, March 1962
'Latter Day Pinter' in *Drama Survey*, Winter 1964

Dukore, Bernard   'The Theatre of Harold Pinter' in *Tulane Drama Review*, March 1962.

Hoefer, Jacqueline   'Pinter and Whiting: Two Attitudes towards the Alienated Arist' in *Modern Drama*, February 1962

Knight, Wilson   'The Kitchen Sink' in *Encounter*, December 1963

Lahr, John   'Pinter the Spaceman' in *Evergreen Review*, No. 55, June 1968

Morris, Kelly   'The Homecoming' in *Tulane Drama Review*, Winter 1966

Schechner, Richard   'Puzzling Pinter' in *Tulane Drama Review*, Winter 1966

Bibliography
Gordon, Lois G.   'Pigeonholing Pinter: A Bibliography', Theatre Documentation, Fall 1968

PERFORMANCES

April 1958	*The Birthday Party* at the Arts, Cambridge, transferring to the Lyric, Hammersmith, directed by Peter Wood with Richard Pearson
July 1959	*A Slight Ache* on the BBC Third Programme directed by Donald McWhinnie with Maurice Denham
January 1960	*The Room* with Vivien Merchant and *The Dumb Waiter* with George Tovey and Nicholas Selby at the Hampstead Theatre Club, transferring to the Royal Court
March 1960	*A Night Out* on the BBC Third Programme directed by Donald McWhinnie with Barry Foster and
April 1960	on ABC Television's Armchair Theatre directed by Philip Saville with Tom Bell
April 1960	*The Caretaker* at the Arts directed by Donald McWhinnie with Donald Pleasence
January 1961	*A Slight Ache* at the Arts directed by Donald McWhinnie with Emlyn Williams
May 1961	*The Collection* televised by Associated-Rediffusion directed by Joan Kemp-Welch with John Ronane, Anthony Bate and Griffith Jones and
June 1962	staged at the Aldwych directed by Peter Hall and Harold Pinter with John Ronane, Kenneth Haigh and Michael Hordern
March 1963	*The Lover* televised by Associated-Rediffusion directed by Joan Kemp-Welch with Vivien Merchant and Alan Badel
September 1963	*The Lover* staged at the Arts directed by Harold Pinter with Vivien Merchant and Scott Forbes

Harold Pinter

March 1965 | *Tea Party* televised by the BBC directed by Charles Jarrott with Leo McKern

June 1965 | *The Homecoming* at the Aldwych directed by Peter Hall with Paul Rogers and Michael Bryant

February 1967 | *The Basement* televised by the BBC directed by Charles Jarrott with Derek Godfrey, Harold Pinter and Kika Markham

April 1968 | *Landscape* on the BBC Third Programme directed by Guy Vaesen with Dame Peggy Ashcroft and Eric Porter

July 1969 | *Landscape* and *Silence* at the Aldwych Theatre directed by Peter Hall with Dame Peggy Ashcroft

September 1970 | *Tea Party* and *The Basement* at the Duchess directed by James Hammerstein with Donald Pleasence, Vivien Merchant, Barry Foster and Stephanie Beacham

June 1971 | *Old Times* at the Aldwych directed by Peter Hall with Colin Blakely, Dorothy Tutin and Vivien Merchant

1972 | Wrote a preliminary screenplay for Joseph Losey based on Proust's *A la recherche du temps perdu*

April 1973 | *Monologue* televised by the BBC directed by Christopher Morahan with Henry Woolf, who played the part on stage later in the year at two fringe theatres: The Orange Tree, Richmond and The King's Head, Islington

FILMOGRAPHY

The Caretaker

Screenplay written 1962. Film shot in a derelict house in Hackney 1962–63, directed by Clive Donner, with Donald Pleasence, Alan Bates and Robert Shaw. Budget: about £30,000. First screening: Berlin Film Festival, June 1963. Shown in New York in January 1954 under the title *The Guest*. Distributors in UK: British Lion

The Servant

Screenplay written 1962. Film shot on location in London and at Shepperton Studios January–March 1963, directed by Joseph Losey with Dirk Bogarde, James Fox, Sarah Miles and Wendy Craig. First screening: Venice Film Festival, September 1963. Released in UK in November 1963; in US in March 1964. Distributors: Elstree

The Pumpkin Eater

Screenplay written 1963. Film shot on location at St Peter's Square, Hammersmith and at Shepperton Studios September–December 1963, directed by Jack Clayton with Anne Bancroft, Peter Finch, James Mason, Maggie Smith and Richard Johnson. Released in 1964. Distributors: Columbia

The Quiller Memorandum

Screenplay written 1966. Film shot 1966. Directed by Michael Anderson with George Segal, Senta Berger, Max von Sydow and Alec Guinness. Released November 1966. Distributors: The Rank Organization

Accident

Screenplay written 1966. Film shot on location at Cobham, Oxford, London and Syon House and at Twickenham Studios, July–September 1966, directed by Joseph Losey with Dirk Bogarde, Jacqueline Sassard, Stanley Baker, Michael York, Vivien Merchant and Delphine Seyrig. Released in UK February 1967; in US April 1967. Distributors in UK: London Independent Producers Monarch (GB)

Harold Pinter

The Birthday Party

Screenplay written 1968. Film shot at Shepperton Studios, directed by William Friedkin with Robert Shaw, Patrick Magee, Dandy Nichols, Sydney Tafler, Moultrie Kelsall and Helen Fraser. Distributor: Connoisseur Films

The Homecoming

Screenplay written 1968–69 for John Frankenheimer to direct. The project was never realized but it is now possible that Peter Hall will direct the film for Columbia

The Go-Between

Screenplay written 1969. Film shot on location at Melton Constable Hall in Norfolk, July–August 1970. Directed by Joseph Losey with Alan Bates, Julie Christie, Dominic Guard, Margaret Leighton, Michael Redgrave and Michael Gough. Released September 1971. Distributors: EMI/MGM

HAROLD PINTER

No adjectives have been derived from the names of Osborne, Beckett, Whiting or Arden but the words 'Pinterish' or 'Pinteresque' are already familiar, which must mean that his style is the most distinctive, or at least the most easily recognizable.

Pinter has capitalized in a way that no playwright had ever done before – though many have since – on the fact that real-life conversations don't proceed smoothly and logically from point to point. Conventional characters in conventional plays listen to each other intently and answer each other intelligently, but it's only a tiny minority of people who do this in reality. The average everyday conversation is repetitious or inconsequential or both; Pinter has an accurate and affectionate ear for the irrationality of dialogue, and not only working-class dialogue, though it's the working-class characters who make it stand out in the clearest relief, as in the revue sketch *Last to Go*.

> MAN: I went to see if I could get hold of George.
> BARMAN: Who?
> MAN: George.
> (*Pause.*)
> BARMAN: George who?
> MAN: George ... whatsisname.
> BARMAN: Oh.
> (*Pause.*)
> Did you get hold of him?
> MAN: No. No, I couldn't get hold of him. I couldn't locate him.
> BARMAN: He's not about much now, is he?
> (*Pause.*)
> MAN: When did you last see him then?
> BARMAN: Oh, I haven't seen him for years.
> MAN: No, nor me.
> (*Pause.*)
> BARMAN: Used to suffer very bad from arthritis.
> MAN: Arthritis?
> BARMAN: Yes.

Harold Pinter

MAN: He never suffered from arthritis.
BARMAN: Suffered very bad.
(*Pause.*)
MAN: Not when I knew him.
(*Pause.*)
BARMAN: I think he must have left the area.
(*Pause.*)
MAN: Yes, it was the *Evening News* was the last to go to-night.
BARMAN: Not always the last though, is it, though?
MAN: No. Oh no. I mean sometimes it's the *News*. Other times it's one of the others. No way of telling beforehand. Until you've got your last one left, of course. Then you can tell which one it's going to be.
BARMAN: Yes.
(*Pause.*)
MAN: Oh yes.
(*Pause.*)
I think he must have left the area.

This is writing which succeeds by breaking all the rules of writing. It's good because it's so realistically full of bad syntax, tautologies, pleonasms, repetitions, *non sequiturs* and self-contradictions. The characters are not only uninterested in listening; they're hardly interested in what they're saying themselves.

This passage is a fair example of what would be regarded as 'Pinterish'. But in a sense it's unfortunate for a writer when an adjective like this becomes so very common so very soon. It's also misleading, because it suggests that what's typical of him at one stage of his development is also typical of every other, that his style has remained at a standstill.

Pinter's hasn't. We see him using the same tricks of circling repetitious and tangential irrelevancies in the plays, not always to such great comic effect, but more subtly.

DAVIES: I can't move without them papers. They tell you who I am. You see! I'm stuck without them.
ASTON: Why's that?
DAVIES: You see, what it is, you see, I changed my name! Years

ago. I been going around under an assumed name! That's not my real name.

ASTON: What name you been going under?

DAVIES: Jenkins. Bernard Jenkins. That's my name. That's the name I'm known, anyway. But it's no good me going on with that name. I got no rights. I got an insurance card here. (*He takes a card from his pocket.*) Under the name of Jenkins. See? Bernard Jenkins. Look. It's got four stamps on it. Four of them. But I can't go along with these.

Here, Davies's character is shaped largely through the jumping of his grass-hopper mind from one subject to the other, always evading the real point. The rhythm of procrastination can be heard in every sentence he utters. The language has become a function of the character just as the character is a function of the theme. The evasion of points, in action as in speech, is the main subject of the play.

Pinter's earlier plays are closer to the revue sketch in style. The repetitiveness, the inconsequentiality and the irrationality are served up as objects of interest in themselves.

MR KIDD: . . . She's been dead some time now, my sister. It was a good house then. She was a capable woman. Yes. Fine size of a woman too. I think she took after my mum. Yes, I think she took after my old mum, from what I can recollect. I think my mum was a Jewess. Yes, I wouldn't be surprised to learn that she was a Jewess. She didn't have many babies.

ROSE: What about your sister, Mr Kidd?

MR KIDD: What about her?

ROSE: Did she have any babies?

MR KIDD: Yes, she had a resemblance to my old mum, I think. Taller, of course.

ROSE: When did she die then, your sister?

MR KIDD: Yes, that's right, it was after she died that I must have stopped counting. She used to keep things in very good trim.

Here he is already exploring new areas of verbal comedy, but later as the technique is refined, there is a more subtly humorous enjoyment in the weird progressions of the characters' thoughts. The

3

non-sequiturs in Meg's speech at Stanley's birthday party show up the ghastliness of her sentimentality with a searchlight clarity, which is both remorseless and affectionate.

> Well – it's very, very nice to be here tonight, in my house, and I want to propose a toast to Stanley, because it's his birthday, and he's lived here for a long while now, and he's my Stanley now. And I think he's a good boy, although sometimes he's bad. (*An appreciative laugh from Goldberg.*) And he's the only Stanley I know, and I know him better than all the world, although he doesn't think so. ('*Hear – hear*' *from Goldberg.*) Well, I could cry because I'm so happy, having him here and not gone away, on his birthday, and there isn't anything I wouldn't do for him, and all you good people here tonight . . . (*She sobs.*)

And in *The Collection,* the technique is still further developed with a new and acid precision in the tersely economic interlocution. Each repetition and variation has its point.

> HARRY: What a beautiful lamp.
> STELLA: What can I do for you?
> HARRY: Do you know Bill Lloyd?
> STELLA: No.
> HARRY: Oh, you don't?
> STELLA: No.
> HARRY: You don't know him personally?
> STELLA: I don't, no.
> HARRY: I found him in a slum, you know, by accident. Just happened to be in a slum one day and there he was. I realized he had talent straight away. I gave him a roof, gave him a job, and he came up trumps. We've been close friends for years.
> STELLA: Oh yes?
> HARRY: You know of him, of course, don't you, by repute? He's a dress designer.
> STELLA: I know of him.
> HARRY: You're both dress designers.
> STELLA: Yes.
> HARRY: You don't belong to the Rags and Bags Club, do you?
> STELLA: The what?
> HARRY: The Rags and Bags Club. I thought I might have seen you down there.

STELLA: No, I don't know it.
HARRY: Shame. You'd like it.
(*Pause*).
    Yes.
(*Pause.*)
    I've come about your husband.

Here the inconsequentiality is harnessed not only to the characterization, as it was with Davies and with Meg, but also to the elabora-
tion of the situation. Harry is tense because he is suspicious of
Bill's relationship with Stella and he is revenging himself on her by
deliberately confusing her. The inconsequentiality has become a
sadistic weapon in the hands of a character who knows what he's
doing with it.

One point that Pinter has in common with Osborne is that they
both specialize in one-sided dialogues. But they do so in very different
ways. The on-stage listeners during Jimmy Porter's monologues (or
Archie Rice's or Luther's) are very unimportant. In Pinter the
unbalance in the number of words spoken is often just as great.
Time and again we get a nagging mother figure like Meg or Rose in
The Room or the woman in *A Night Out* doing practically all the
talking while the husband or son or lodger preserves a protracted
silence. But Pinter is far from identifying with the speaker. His
focus is always on the fact of unbalance. He's just as interested in
the listener – even if he isn't listening – as in the speaker. He seems
to have no difficulty in achieving this detachment: it seems natural
for him to stand very much farther back from his subject than
Osborne does. In *The Homecoming*, when Ruth asks Teddy whether
the family has read his 'critical works', his answer goes a long way
towards defining Pinter's own position – that of standing outside the
event as an observer.

You wouldn't understand my works. You wouldn't have the
faintest idea of what they were about. You wouldn't appreciate
the points of reference. You're way behind. All of you. There's no
point in my sending you my works. You'd be lost. It's nothing to
do with the question of intelligence. It's a way of being able to
look at the world. It's a question of how far you can operate on
things and not in things. I mean it's a question of your capacity

to ally the two, to relate the two, to balance the two. To see, to be able to *see*! I'm the one who can see. That's why I can write my critical works. Might do you good ... have a look at them ... see how certain people can view ... things ... how certain people can maintain ... intellectual equilibrium. Intellectual equilibrium. You're just objects. You just ... move about. I can observe it. I can see what you do. It's the same as I do. But you're lost in it. You won't get me being ... I won't be lost in it.

No doubt the detachment is an indispensable prerequisite for the accuracy with which Pinter hears and records dialogue. Osborne is a writer who readily commits himself, and not only on political issues. He writes like a good talker and a bad listener. Pinter, who is very loth to commit himself, writes like a compulsive listener.

BARBARA: What did he say then?
SALLY: Come over with me one Sunday, he says, come over and have Sunday dinner, meet the wife. Why, I said, what are you going to introduce me as, your sister? No, he says, she's very broadminded, my wife, she'll be delighted to meet you.
MAVIS: Oh yes, I've heard of that kind of thing before.
SALLY: Yes, that's what I said. Oh yes, I said, I've heard of that kind of thing before. Go on, get off out of it, I said, buzz off before I call a copper.
BARBARA: Which was he, the one with the big nose?
SALLY: Yes.

The night-club hostesses in *Night School* don't interest Pinter particularly but he still shows a delight in getting the words and the rhythms right. He's equally effective in completely differing social contexts, but his favourite locales are all-night coffee stalls, transport cafés and milk bars.

SECOND OLD WOMAN: Did you see that one come up and speak to me at the counter?
FIRST: Who?
SECOND: Comes up to me, he says, hullo, he says, what's the time by your clock? Bloody liberty. I was just standing there getting your soup.
FIRST: It's tomato soup.
SECOND: What's the time by your clock? he says.
FIRST: I bet you answered him back.

SECOND: I told him all right. Go on, I said, why don't you get back into your scraghole, I said, clear off out of it before I call a copper.

But he's also master of Edward's idiom in *A Slight Ache*.

You must excuse my chatting away like this. We have few visitors this time of the year. All our friends summer abroad. I'm a home bird myself. Wouldn't mind taking a trip to Asia Minor, mind you, or to certain lower regions of the Congo, but Europe? Out of the question. Much too noisy. I'm sure you agree.

In developing a style which is flexible as this, realistic and yet stylized, and capable of covering such a wide social and emotional range, Pinter's achievement has been enormous. But his limitations are also enormous, stemming partly from the detachment. He isn't interested in exploring experience. Basically his vision of the world remains a child's-eye view. He's obsessed with the subject of the safety of the womb or room and the dangers of dispossession. Many of the men in his work are either dispossessors or dispossessed and almost all the women are either possessive mother figures or tarts – and so almost impossible to possess. Some are both. Not one is sympathetic. Most are garrulous. Rose, in *The Room*, talks incessantly. There are no women in *The Dumb Waiter*, and in *The Birthday Party* there are Meg, who chatters non-stop to her husband and makes her lodger into a substitute son-cum-lover, and Lulu, who isn't a tart but may end up as one. In *A Slight Ache*, the wife finally gives herself to the matchseller and presents her husband with the old man's match-tray. In *A Night Out* we have the nagging mother and the flirty office girls, who lead Albert on. There are no women in *The Caretaker* and in *Night School* the nagging mother role is divided between the two aunts and a school-teacher who turns out to be a night-club hostess. *The Dwarfs* has no women in it; the woman in *The Collection* is a brittle enigma; the woman in *The Lover* has to play at being unfaithful, though actually she isn't; the two main women in *Tea Party* are both enigmatic and unsympathetic; and in *The Homecoming* the ex-tart is quite willing to go back to being a tart again. It's certainly an extraordinary series of parts that Pinter has written for women, and it is interesting that when a woman interviewer told him that she found none of his characters likable, the

Harold Pinter

women especially being 'extremely feminine in a rather cruel and taunting way', his reply was that he liked them all very much himself and that the women weren't all wicked or all awful from his point of view. But in his determination to 'operate on things and not in things' he seems to rein himself back from involvement in his characters' experience, and the women come off far worse than the men

Not that the men get much sympathy. Davies and Aston come off best. Though acutely aware of everything that stops them from functioning properly, Pinter identifies with them considerably and they both emerge quite strongly in three dimensions, Davies more than Aston.

But Pinter's whole method of characterization differs sharply from the conventional method we're used to, which derives from Ibsen. For Ibsen, the past histories of the characters are the soil in which the whole plot is planted. For Pinter, the past histories of the characters, like their off-stage lives and their social backgrounds, couldn't matter less. The only facts that he's concerned with are the facts of what is said and done on stage. In *The Birthday Party,* we only know Stanley's past as he describes it. But there is no interest in getting at the truth behind his falsifications. What's important is that he is falsifying. The focus is always on the here-and-now.

This does not prevent the characters or the social settings from creating a very definite impression. The cheap seaside boarding house of *The Birthday Party* and the room full of accumulated junk in *The Caretaker* strike us as very real, and Goldberg and Meg are both solid characters, though Pinter doesn't tell us much about them. Neither of them is really more than the incarnation of a line of talk. They both 'do' things but their actions don't help much to define them. In fact the extent to which they succeed as 'characters' shows how little characters need to be defined. None of Pinter's characters are defined by their past history (which they're liable to distort), their position in society (which they're liable to misrepresent), their attitudes (which are inconsistent) or by their physical appearance (which is seldom described). Generally, we know nothing about them, except what we see and hear for ourselves, and their statements are often self-contradictory and their actions inconsistent.

In withholding from his audiences the clear bounding lines of the definition that he knows they crave for, Pinter is pursuing a deliberate policy.

> The desire for verification is understandable, but cannot always be satisfied. There are no hard distinctions between what is real and what is unreal, nor between what is true and what false. The thing is not necessarily either true or false; it can be both true and false. The assumption that to verify what has happened and what is happening presents no problems, I take to be inaccurate. A character on the stage who can present no convincing argument or information as to his past experiences, his present behaviour or his aspirations, nor give a comprehensive analysis of his motives is as legitimate and as worthy of attention as one who, alarmingly, can do all these things. The more acute the experience the less articulate its expression.

Pinter's story-line is usually subject to the same indefiniteness as his characters. We are often in doubt about whether an event has really taken place or not because we're never sure whether to believe the characters. Before Pinter and before the other writers in what Martin Esslin has dubbed the Theatre of the Absurd, we could always take it for granted that what a character said on stage was true, unless we were given specific reasons for distrusting him. Pinter cuts right through this convention. In his first play, *The Room,* Mr Kidd is made to prattle on at great length about his sister but as soon as he goes out of the room, Rose says, 'I don't believe he had a sister, ever.'

Most drama is built up out of addition. Points are planted one by one until they add up to a plot. Pinter's method often works by subtraction. He plants a point only to uproot it, without ever going into the character's motivations for misrepresenting the reality. So the impossibility of verifying reality becomes not only a source of suspense but one of the fundamental subjects of his plays.

The plays are thrillers, full of mysteries that are put in with no intention of solving them and no pretence that the playwright himself is in a position to. They work on the audience by spreading out the mystification, enjoying it and exploring it for its own sake but never resolving it. Hints are dropped deliberately as if they were clues in the mystery but the trail of evidence never leads to a solution. Up to *The Collection,* the element of mystification is kept fairly well under control, used as a valid ingredient in the play. After *The Lover,* however, what had been a means becomes an end, and the quality of the work suffers. Sometimes, as in *Tea Party,* his most obscure television play, he uses it in a rather unfair way to titillate the audience's appetite without ever satisfying it. But in the earlier, more controlled plays, the element of mystification is used with more justification.

The Room is full of mysteries. In *The Dumb Waiter* we never find out much about the set-up that organizes the murders or why Gus has to be killed. *The Birthday Party* never explains what is behind the take-over bid Goldberg and McCann make for possession of Stanley. In *A Slight Ache,* the motivations of the matchseller are a mystery which torment Edward, who cannot understand why he should stand there day after day, where nobody ever passes, never selling a single box. But for us, the focus is not on the mystery of the old man but on why Edward and Flora react to him in the way they do, as if he were a threat to them. In *The Caretaker,* Mick's teasing enjoyment of violence as a kind of practical joke builds up a great deal of effective stage terror. but his motivations remain nearly as obscure as those of Goldberg and McCann, who may be under orders, as they say they are, but in neither case do we get an explanation. Motives aren't important either for Pinter or for us. In *The Collection,* the whole play hinges on a mystery – what happened in Leeds when Bill and Stella stayed in the same hotel? Did they sleep together or just kiss in the corridor or just sit in the lounge and talk? As the play shows, it doesn't really matter what has happened. What matters is what happens out of it, in the here-and-now. Once an action is in the past tense, there's no way of distinguishing fact from fiction. The two mix together, like hot and cold water in a bath.

THE ROOM

The Room was written early in 1957 and first staged by the Drama Department of Bristol University, but it wasn't given a professional production until the Hampstead Theatre Club put it on in January 1960.

It gives a first airing to many of the preoccupations which have since become familiar from Pinter's other plays. Rose isn't a mother, but she's the prototype of all Pinter's chattering, fussing, nagging mother-figures, the women who never stop to listen but never stop asking implicitly for the goodwill of the husband or son or nephew or lodger. The play opens with a long scene in which Bert (who's at the table with his cap on and a magazine propped up in front of him) eats, drinks and reads, without uttering a word, while Rose prattles on about the food she's giving him and how cold it is outside and how lucky they are to have such a nice room. By talking in the way she does, she's giving herself the reassurance which he refuses to give her. If she asks a question, she either answers it herself or goes on about something else without giving him time to answer, even if he wanted to. But she knows he doesn't and she's basically insulting him in exactly the same way that he's insulting her: by ignoring him. She's talking to him all the time but disregarding his refusal to react, which is itself a reaction. She's treating him like a little boy, telling him to put on a thick jersey, and she tells him what he thinks and feels, as if she knows better than he does. Her existence is centred on his but in effect she's denying him the right or the ability to exist independently. In many ways her behaviour corresponds to what Ronald Laing* calls 'schizophrenogenic' – i.e. liable to undermine the man's confidence in his own emotional reactions and his own perception of reality. Bert gives no sign of being vulnerable and Pinter gives no sign of being interested in whether he is or not, but Rose's behaviour pattern is almost exactly the same as Meg's in *The Birthday Party* and the mother's in *A Night Out*. In each case, the woman wants to keep the man in the house, in her sphere of influence and in her routine, although she pretends not to mind whether he goes out.

I haven't been out. I haven't been so well. I didn't feel up to it.

* R. D. Laing: *The Self and Others* (Tavistock).

Still, I'm much better today. I don't know about you though. I don't know whether you ought to go out. I mean, you shouldn't, straight after you've been laid up. Still. Don't worry, Bert. You go. You won't be long.

Then a minute later:

I don't know why you have to go out. Couldn't you run it down tomorrow? I could put the fire in later. You could sit by the fire. That's what you like, Bert, of an evening. It'll be dark in a minute as well, soon.

From the very first line of her monologue, there's great emphasis on the cold and the dark and the dangers of the world outside compared to the safety and comfort of the room. Rose isn't only afraid of the world outside the house but nervous about other people in other rooms. She doesn't know whether anyone has moved into the basement and obviously hopes that no one has.

I don't know who lives down there now. Whoever it is, they're taking a big chance. Maybe they're foreigners.

Having established her insecurity, Pinter meticulously builds up an atmosphere of uncertainty and vagueness around her and around the room. The room itself is unambiguous – it's like the here-and-now, we can see it – but we don't know which floor it's on and Mr Kidd doesn't know how many floors there are in the house, and then we don't know for sure whether Mr Kidd is the landlord or not. Rose says he is but Mr and Mrs Sands say he isn't. Mr Kidd also contradicts himself about whether the house is full or not and he's evasive about which room he lives in himself. At one time he used to live in this room but he won't say or doesn't remember how long ago that was. The elaborate vagueness about time and place is very reminiscent of *Waiting for Godot,* and so is the rhythm of the dialogue with its staccato and its monosyllables.

MRS SANDS: Why don't you sit down, Mrs —
ROSE: Hudd. No thanks.
MR SANDS: What did you say?
ROSE: When?
MR SANDS: What did you say the name was?
ROSE: Hudd.
MR SANDS: That's it. You're the wife of the bloke you mentioned then?

MRS SANDS: No, she isn't. That was Mr Kidd.
MR SANDS: Was it? I thought it was Hudd.
MRS SANDS: No, it was Kidd. Wasn't it, Mrs Hudd?
ROSE: That's right. The landlord.
MRS SANDS: No, not the landlord. The other man.
ROSE: Well, that's his name. He's the landlord.
MR SANDS: Who?
ROSE: Mr Kidd.
(*Pause.*)
MR SANDS: Is he?
MRS SANDS: Maybe there are two landlords.
(*Pause.*)
MR SANDS: That'll be the day.
MRS SANDS: What did you say?
MR SANDS: I said that'll be the day.
(*Pause.*)
ROSE: What's it like out?
MRS SANDS: It's very dark out.
MR SANDS: No darker than in.
MRS SANDS: He's right there.
MR SANDS: It's darker in than out, for my money.

The repetitiousness, the short and sometimes meaningful names (like Kidd) and the way the dialogue tacks back on itself obviously owe a great deal to Beckett, and Pinter has acknowledged the influence. But he starts to develop a distinctive style of his own in which the questions and answers don't meet each other squarely. Quite apart from the comic effect, the way that the characters continue their own lines of thought shows us what their preoccupations are.

ROSE: Well, it's a shame you have to go out in this weather, Mr Kidd. Don't you have a help?
MR KIDD: Eh?
ROSE: I thought you had a woman to help.
MR KIDD: I haven't got any woman.
ROSE: I thought you had one when we first came.
MR KIDD: No women here.
ROSE: Maybe I was thinking of somewhere else.
MR KIDD: Plenty of women round the corner. Not here though. Oh no. Eh, have I seen that before?
ROSE: What?

13

MR KIDD: That.

ROSE: I don't know. Have you?

MR KIDD: I seem to have some remembrance.

ROSE: It's just an old rocking chair.

MR KIDD: Was it here when you came?

ROSE: No, I brought it myself.

MR KIDD: I could swear blind I've seen that before.

ROSE: Perhaps you have.

MR KIDD: What?

ROSE: I say, perhaps you have.

MR KIDD: Yes, maybe I have.

ROSE: Take a seat, Mr Kidd.

MR KIDD: I wouldn't take an oath on it though.

It's also characteristic of Pinter to make the woman into the spokesman for static security. What she voices is the desire to stay where she is in space and time. She's safe and satisfied with things as they are. When the blind Negro comes up from the basement, where he's been waiting for her with a message from her father, this is an invitation to make a movement back into the past. 'Come home, Sal.' The appearance of the blind Negro from the basement is more overtly symbolical than anything else in Pinter's work, although the meaning is open to any number of interpretations. Is the Negro the same man that Mr and Mrs Sands met in the dark and who told them that room Number 7 was vacant? Why does Rose start off by claiming that she doesn't know him and then seem to know that his name isn't Riley? And why does he call her Sal? (This is only the first of several instances in Pinter's plays where characters go by more than one name, suggesting that nothing is constant about their identity.) Why does Rose go blind when Bert kicks the Negro's head against the gas stove? This final episode in the play bristles with even more insoluble mysteries than the earlier episodes. Was Mr Sands perching or sitting on the table? Why does Mrs Sands object to this? Were the Sands going up or down the stairs when Rose opened the door of her room?

In each case the question is unanswerable on the evidence Pinter gives us but in each case the fact that it's unanswerable contributes to the dramatic effect. This is a technique that Pinter went on using but his ways of using it were soon to become much subtler.

THE DUMB WAITER

The Dumb Waiter, his next one-act play, is a much more accomplished and relaxed piece of writing. The mystification is more controlled and the doors are open to much more comedy. The technique draws from both Beckett and from music hall. Elaborate routines and stage business are mapped out and very funny dialogue is built up out of irrelevant scraps of information.

GUS *ties his laces, rises, yawns and begins to walk slowly to the door, left. He stops, looks down, and shakes his foot.*

BEN *lowers his paper and watches him.* GUS *kneels and unties his shoe-lace and slowly takes off the shoe. He looks inside it and brings out a flattened matchbox. He shakes it and examines it. Their eyes meet.* BEN *rattles his paper and reads.* GUS *puts the matchbox in his pocket and bends down to put on his shoe. He ties his lace, with difficulty.* BEN *lowers his paper and watches him.* GUS *walks to the door, left, stops, and shakes the other foot. He kneels, unties his shoe-lace, and slowly takes off the shoe. He looks inside it and brings out a flattened cigarette packet. He shakes it and examines it. Their eyes meet.* BEN *rattles his paper and reads.* GUS *puts the packet in his pocket, bends down, puts on his shoe and ties the lace . . .*

BEN: Kaw!
(He picks up the paper.)
What about this? Listen to this!
(He refers to the paper.)
A man of eighty-seven wanted to cross the road. But there was a lot of traffic, see? He couldn't see how he was going to squeeze through. So he crawled under a lorry.
GUS: He what?
BEN: He crawled under a lorry. A stationary lorry.
GUS: No?
BEN: The lorry started and ran over him.
GUS: Go on!
BEN: That's what it says here.
GUS: Get away.

15

Harold Pinter

BEN: It's enough to make you want to puke, isn't it?
GUS: Who advised him to do a thing like that?
BEN: A man of eighty-seven crawling under a lorry!
GUS: It's unbelievable.
BEN: It's down here in black and white.
GUS: Incredible.

This is how the play begins: instead of planting points to get the plot going, Pinter is quite content to lean back and let the characters chat. He goes on to use the ballcock in the lavatory system, memories of football matches seen years ago and three-quarters forgotten, and more fragments read out of newspapers. But the comic touches aren't there just for their own sake. Underneath the casual surface, the components for an odd kind of plot are being assembled. We gather that Ben and Gus are here to do a job, but Pinter is in no hurry to let us know that they're professional killers. The crisp brightness of the comedy is being enjoyed in the unpleasant shadow of an impending climax of violence.

Again, the mystification contributes to the atmosphere and the flavour of what's going on. The men themselves seem to know comparatively little about the organization they're working for, though we never know quite how much they know. Complaining that there's no wireless in the room, Gus says:

He doesn't seem to bother much about our comfort these days.

But we have no idea who 'he' is. 'He' is rather like 'they' in Beckett – the power that's responsible for making things the way they are and putting the protagonists into the situation that they're in, but anonymous and unfathomable.

In fact the whole conception of the play seems to owe a great deal to Beckett's novel *Molloy*. The pattern is the same – two men, one with authority over the other, in pursuit of a third man – and in both plots the quantity of unknown facts is overwhelming. Moran, the 'agent' in *Molloy*, knows little about the organization that he's working for, and much of the comedy hinges on the discrepancy between the gravity of the mission (vague though it is) and the triviality of the distractions that get in the way of carrying it out. In *The Dumb Waiter*, Ben and Gus know what they have to do, but they don't know why, they don't know who their victims are and they don't know what advantage their deaths are to the organization that employs them. But the curiosity they show is fairly perfunctory: we don't feel that they really want to know any more than they do.

> GUS: Who clears up after we've gone? I'm curious about that. Who does the clearing up? Maybe they don't clear up. Maybe they just leave them there, eh? What do you think? How many jobs have we done? Blimey, I can't count them. What if they never clear anything up after we've gone.
> BEN (*pityingly*): You mutt. Do you think we're the only branch of this organization? Have a bit of common. They got departments for everything.
> GUS: What cleaners and all?
> BEN: You birk!

Their willingness to obey orders without inquiring into the mysteries behind them is bizarrely but amusingly underlined when the dumb waiter of the title starts to work. At first it had seemed that the room, as in *The Room,* was a place for resting and safety. But when the matches are slid underneath the door, Ben and Gus know that they are not alone in the house, and when they suddenly hear a loud clattering sound in the wall between the beds they panic and grab their revolvers – and then the tension is punctured beautifully when the two men read the piece of paper they take out of the dumb waiter.

> GUS: Two braised steak and chips. Two sago puddings. Two teas without sugar.
> BEN: Let me see that. (*He takes the paper.*)
> GUS (*To himself*): Two teas without sugar.

The gunmen's pathetic efforts to obey the orders that come out of the shaft provide some moments of high comedy, especially when they reply to the demand for 'Macaroni Pastitsio' and 'Ormitha Macarounada' with three McVitie and Price biscuits, a packet of Lyons Red Label tea, a packet of Smith's Crisps and an Eccles cake, a half-pint of milk and a bar of Cadbury's fruit and nut chocolate. (Pinter shares the pleasure Beckett takes in cataloguing details into lists.) The situation is as bizarre as anything in *The*

17

Room but the symbolism is much less insistent. In a sense, the man who remains unseen and gives orders from above becomes like God, especially when Ben and Gus send up all they have, and he still isn't satisfied. But there is enough comedy to prevent the symbolism from overbalancing the play and the unsolved mysteries don't prevent the final twist (when it turns out that Gus is to be the victim) from being neat and theatrically satisfying.

THE BIRTHDAY PARTY

The Birthday Party was presented in May 1958 by Michael Codron at the Lyric, Hammersmith, where it bewildered the critics of the daily papers and had already been taken off before *The Sunday Times* appeared with a glowing review by Harold Hobson. . . . 'Mr Pinter, on the evidence of this work, possesses the most original, disturbing and arresting talent in theatrical London.' The play was revived in May 1959 by the Tavistock Repertory Company at the Tower Theatre. Thanks to the magazine *Encore* this amateur production was seen by a great many people who would otherwise have missed it, and it helped to turn the tide in Pinter's direction. Pinter himself pronounced the production better than the Hammersmith one. Certainly it was better than his own very slow production of the play for the Royal Shakespeare Company in June 1964.

It has more substance than either of his other full-length plays. The impact is enormous, with moments of terror and violence on the stage that are the best Pinter has contrived, while the structure is the most impressive he's yet achieved. The parts all contribute to the whole and the comedy blends well with the serious statements. The mystification is there, as always, but it doesn't interfere with the precision and clarity of the pattern.

It's been objected that Goldberg and McCann are less realistic than the other characters. Certainly they're less rooted into the realistic context of the shabby seaside boarding house and certainly they're more mysterious than Meg and Petey and Lulu, because we don't know what they're at. Like Ben and Gus, they're two agents working for some organization we know nothing about, but although their mission and its motives remain mysterious, their language and their behaviour merge perfectly well into the rest of the play.

Stanley, who is clearly a 'naturalistic character' in that he isn't sent from another world, as they seem to be, is in fact just as impenetrable as they are. Except for what we see of his lethargy, we are given no idea what's made him into the failure he is today. We know very little about his past, except for the hints of some estrangement from his father, but, like Goldberg and McCann, he's convincing

Harold Pinter

without being entirely understandable. Like all Pinter's characters, he exists entirely through what he says and does on stage, but this existence is quite sufficient.

The beginning of the play is very much like that of *The Room*, with Petey sitting at the breakfast-table with a paper, while Meg prattles on with her suffocating mixture of motherly attentiveness and self-praise. She seems to think her cornflakes are nicer than anybody else's. When Stanley, the substitute child for this childless mother, comes down, late, to breakfast, the flirty game that Meg plays with him is full of the affectionate insults that Pinter is so good at writing.

> MEG (*shyly*): Am I really succulent?
>
> STANLEY: Oh, you are. I'd rather have you than a cold in the nose any day.
>
> MEG: You're just saying that.
>
> STANLEY (*violently*): Look, why don't you get this place cleared up! It's a pigsty. And another thing, what about my room? It needs sweeping. I need a new room!
>
> MEG (*sensual, stroking his arm*): Oh, Stan, that's a lovely room. I've had some lovely afternoons in that room.

But the enjoyment of this squalid idyll is shattered in the usual Pinterish way – the safety of the room is threatened by the prospect of intruders from the world outside. Stanley, like a child, is immediately scared when he hears that Meg is expecting visitors and he gets his own back by scaring her.

> STANLEY (*advancing*): They're coming today.
>
> MEG: Who?
>
> STANLEY: They're coming in a van.
>
> MEG: Who?
>
> STANLEY: And do you know what they've got in that van?
>
> MEG: What?
>
> STANLEY: They've got a wheelbarrow in that van.
>
> MEG (*breathlessly*): They haven't.
>
> STANLEY: Oh yes they have.
>
> MEG: You're a liar.
>
> STANLEY (*advancing upon her*): A big wheelbarrow. And when the van stops they wheel it out, and they wheel it up the garden path, and then they knock at the front door.

20

MEG: They don't.
STANLEY: They're looking for someone.
MEG: They're not.
STANLEY: They're looking for someone. A certain person.
MEG (*hoarsely*): No, they're not!
STANLEY: Shall I tell you who they're looking for?
MEG: No!

This is almost like a prophecy of doom in a Greek tragedy. We have no idea whether Stanley has any reason for being so anxious, but the dialogue builds up the expectation that something pretty nasty is going to happen.

The scene with Meg contains several indications of Stanley's immaturity. He puts up with her fussy mothering, which even goes to the extreme of asking him 'Did you pay a visit this morning?' and he obviously wants to do nothing but lie in bed and sit indoors, like a child afraid of going to school. His scene with Lulu carries the suggestion of immaturity still further. The girl is obviously willing to be interested in him, in spite of her complaints about his not washing or shaving, but he turns down the chance she gives him of going out with her. He doesn't want to go out at all.

The Stanley–Lulu scene is followed by the first scene with Goldberg and McCann – the Jew and the Irishman of the traditional joke. Goldberg's character immediately makes a very strong impact. He talks about himself with all the self-satisfaction of a self-made man and hands out glib advice to anyone who will listen – or seem to – with a vulgarly paternal expansiveness.

GOLDBERG: Sit back, McCann. Relax. What's the matter with you? I bring you down for a few days to the seaside. Take a holiday. Do yourself a favour. Learn to relax, McCann, or you'll never get anywhere.
MCCANN: Ah sure I do try, Nat.
GOLDBERG (*sitting at the table, right*): The secret is breathing. Take my tip. It's a well-known fact. Breathe in, breathe out, take a chance, let yourself go. What can you lose? Look at me. When I was an apprentice yet, McCann, every second Friday of the month my Uncle Barney used to take me to the seaside, regular as clockwork. Brighton, Canvey Island, Rottingdean – Uncle Barney wasn't particular. After lunch

Harold Pinter

> on Shabbuss we'd go and sit in a couple of deck-chairs – you
> know, the ones with canopies – we'd have a little paddle, we'd
> watch the tide coming in, going out, the sun coming down
> – golden days, believe me, McCann. (*Reminiscent.*) Uncle Bar-
> ney. Of course, he was an impeccable dresser. One of the old
> school. He had a house just outside Basingstoke at the time.
> Respected by the whole community. Culture ? Don't talk to me
> about culture. He was an all-round man, what do you mean ?
> He was a cosmopolitan.

The inconsequentiality, the enjoyment of place-names, the cheap
joviality, the accuracy of the Jewish rhythms and the proud and
pointless story-telling about relations or acquaintances are typical
of Pinter. So far as his manner of speaking is concerned, Goldberg
might have been created by any of the Jewish writers – even Wolf
Mankowitz – but the association of the familiar manner with the
obscure function is characteristic of Pinter. We don't know whether
Stanley is going to be killed or not, but the way Goldberg speaks
about 'doing the job' reminds us of the two gunmen in *The Dumb
Waiter*, while the way he speaks about how he was given the job is
reminiscent of *Molloy*.

> GOLDBERG: And then this job came up out of the blue. Natur-
> ally they approached me to take care of it. And you know
> who I asked for ?
> MCCANN: Who ?
> GOLDBERG: You.

As in *The Dumb Waiter*, the build-up of mystification develops a
suspense which knocks the comedy into a minor key and, again as
in *The Dumb Waiter*, the symbolism is redeemed from crudeness by
its effectiveness in providing comic relief from the suspense. Meg's
birthday present of a toy drum has several different kinds of sig-
nificance. It sums up the old woman's attitude to the substitute son
who can't bear her but hasn't got the strength to escape. Like Rose's
chatter to Bert, Meg's fussy attentiveness shows the wish to give and
receive attention, combined with an insulting reduction of the grown
man to the status of a little boy. The present of a toy is an ingenuous
attempt to give to the failed musician something that will make up

for his not having a piano, and in giving it she ingenuously asks for a kiss. Stanley's shoulders sag as he complies. To please her, he puts the drum round his neck and beats it, marching round the table. But he loses control and starts banging it frantically as the curtain comes down on Act One.

Act Two, it's clear, will culminate in the actual party but the suspense is built up slowly before we get to it. Some of the things that happen are not at all sinister in themselves but they all add to the accumulation of tensions which will have to break, like a storm, before the play is over. Seemingly to amuse himself, McCann tears a sheet of newspaper into vertical strips, and then, when Stanley isn't allowed to touch the paper, we can't help wondering why. His scene with McCann is full of hidden menace, with odd little touches like having each of them whistle alternate snatches of a tune while the other speaks, so that the whistling is continuous through several lines of dialogue. When Stanley tries to leave, McCann forces him to stay, without actually using any violence, but indicating that he will if necessary. Stanley's guilt and anxiety are very cleverly sketched in, creating some doubt in our minds about whether Goldberg and McCann are intrinsically dangerous to him or, like the match-seller, in *A Slight Ache,* only dangerous because he thinks they are. He makes a pathetic effort, first of all to convince McCann that he isn't the man they're looking for and then, when that fails, to make a friend of him. He also tries to get rid of Goldberg by pretending to be the manager of the boarding house and saying they don't have a room for him.

The scene of rapid-fire questioning seems to owe something to a rather unlikely source: *Johnson Over Jordan,* by J. B. Priestley, which contains a long scene in which the hero is quizzed by two Examiners.

> JOHNSON (*sinking fast now*): Look here, gentlemen, all I can say is – I've tried to do my best.
> 2ND EXAMINER (*going right up to him, in smooth deadly tone*): Possibly. But is your best good enough?
> 1ST EXAMINER (*with the same horrible technique*): After all, what do you *know*?
> 2ND EXAMINER (*severe again now*): How far have you tried to

acquaint yourself with the findings of chemistry, physics, biology, astronomy, mathematics?

1ST EXAMINER: Ask yourself what you know about the Mendelian Law, the Quantum Theory, Spectral Analysis, or the behaviour of Electrons and Neutrons.

2ND EXAMINER: Could you explain Freud's theory of the Id, Marx's Surplus Value, Neo-Realism, Non-representational Art, Polyphonic Music?

1ST EXAMINER: Or – give an exact account of the sequence of events leading up to the outbreak of war in 1914?

2ND EXAMINER (*with dangerous easiness*): You were taught French at school?

JOHNSON: Yes.

2ND EXAMINER (*turning like a tiger*): Have you ever brushed up your French?

The scene in *The Birthday Party* screws the tension still tighter, by making more use of rhythm. But the humour in the lines, which cuts deliberately against the grimness of the bullying, is very reminiscent of the Priestley passage.

GOLDBERG: When did you come to this place?

STANLEY: Last year.

GOLDBERG: Where did you come from?

STANLEY: Somewhere else.

GOLDBERG: Why did you come here?

STANLEY: My feet hurt!

GOLDBERG: Why did you stay?

STANLEY: I had a headache!

GOLDBERG: Did you take anything for it?

STANLEY: Yes.

GOLDBERG: What?

STANLEY: Fruit salts!

GOLDBERG: Enos or Andrews?

STANLEY: En – An —

GOLDBERG: Did you stir properly? Did they fizz?

STANLEY: Now, now, wait, you —

GOLDBERG: Did they fizz? Did they fizz or didn't they fizz?

MCCANN: He doesn't know!

GOLDBERG: You don't know. What's happened to your memory, Webber? When did you last have a bath?

STANLEY: I have one every —
GOLDBERG: Don't lie.
MCCANN: You betrayed the organization. I know him!

The tension is wound up tighter and tighter until it breaks, as it's bound to, into violence. But it isn't the violence we expect. Instead of attacking Stanley, Goldberg is attacked by him, kicked in the stomach, and from the floor he tries to restrain McCann from avenging the blow with a chair he's picked up. As McCann and Stanley face each other, circling, the question is still open whether in cross-questioning Stanley, Goldberg and McCann have been doing anything more sinister than teasing him. Then the scene is interrupted by an off-stage drum-beat. Meg is coming down the stairs in evening dress playing Stanley's toy drum. So now the conflict is forced back out of the open and the menace of impending violence is concealed under the surface of conviviality, as the oddly assorted characters celebrate the birthday party, with Stanley still protesting that it isn't his birthday – a typical Pinter ambiguity.

From its crude presentation in *The Room,* the symbolism of darkness is refined and used with much more theatrical purpose. Stanley can see very little without his glasses, which McCann has snatched off during the interrogation. They're given back to him, but later they're to be broken deliberately. The effect of plunging the stage into darkness and illuminating one face with the beam of a torch is used twice, and after a significant game of blindman's-buff, the stage is in darkness for about two minutes except for a moment when the torch goes on. Grunts from McCann and Goldberg, the noise of a stick banging on the side of the drum and whimpers from Lulu all add to the terror. The build-ups are extremely effective and again when the climaxes of violence come they are not what we expect. At each point of violence or near violence, it's Stanley, who seems so unaggressive, who is the attacker, and it's a woman who is the victim. Before the blackout, blindfold and baited by McCann, with his glasses broken and one foot caught in the broken drum, Stanley tries to strangle Meg. And in the final climax of the act, Lulu is spreadeagled on the table with Stanley bent over her until Goldberg and McCann drive him off. Unfortunately the grudge against women never quite comes into focus either in Stanley or in Pinter.

Harold Pinter

After the suspense, the claustrophobic theatricality and the concentrated multi-level meaningfulness of Act Two, Act Three is something of a let-down. The long opening scene between Meg and Petey is lacking in tension, and without any redeeming comedy. A little suspense is supplied by the big car waiting outside and by the information that Stanley has had a 'nervous breakdown'. The signs are that Goldberg and McCann have got hold of him and that Petey and Meg are powerless to get him out of their clutches. But this is not enough. It's effective when McCann has qualms about going back upstairs into the room where Stanley is and there's a nasty threat in the mention of 'Monty', a friend of Goldberg's, as the doctor best suited to treat Stanley. But altogether the writing lacks the sureness of touch it had in Act Two. There are some comic moments in the scene between Goldberg and McCann, with McCann peering into Goldberg's mouth and Goldberg, who has been bragging about his health, emitting a high-pitched wheeze-whine, which makes him look round as though somebody else had done it. But Pinter doesn't really find his feet until the very funny scene between Lulu and Goldberg.

> LULU (*with growing anger*): You used me for a night. A passing fancy.
> GOLDBERG: Who used who?
> LULU: You made use of me by cunning when my defences were down.
> GOLDBERG: Who took them down?
> LULU: That's what you did. You quenched your ugly thirst. You took advantage of me when I was overwrought. I wouldn't do those things again, not even for a Sultan!
> GOLDBERG: One night doesn't make a harem.
> LULU: You taught me things a girl shouldn't know before she's been married at least three times!
> GOLDBERG: Now you're a jump ahead! What are you complaining about?

The appearance of Stanley provides a very good moment. He's clean-shaven now and dressed in a black jacket and striped trousers with a bowler hat in his hand. (One interpreter concluded that the play was about the conformist pressures of society.) But he can't speak now, only make inarticulate sounds. Goldberg and McCann's scene with him is much less effective than their scene with him in Act Two. The rhythm is strong and the language seems to derive from T. S. Eliot's verse plays – *The Family Reunion* in particular.

GOLDBERG: From now on, we'll be the hub of your wheel.
MCCANN: We'll renew your season ticket.
GOLDBERG: We'll take tuppence off your morning tea.
MCCANN: We'll give you a discount on all inflammable goods.
GOLDBERG: We'll watch over you.
MCCANN: Advise you.

In the end they take him away in the car. Petey, who is one of the very few sympathetic characters in Pinter, tries to stop them, but he's weak and easily scared off by the invitation to come with them. The play ends, as it began, with Meg and Petey alone together, in the room.

A SLIGHT ACHE

A Slight Ache was conceived as a radio play. Commissioned by the BBC for the Third Programme, it was broadcast in July 1959, and put on the stage eighteen months later at the Arts. This is the first of Pinter's plays where the action isn't confined to a single room, but even radio didn't entice him any further afield than the garden, while all the interior action is set in different rooms of the same house. Once again the theme is the threat of the intruder from outside and once again Pinter explores the dramatic potential of silence. But this time it's something different from the silence of the man in face of the nagging woman and from the inarticulacy of the defeated Stanley. In effect, the matchseller's silence is a destructive weapon which enables him to dispossess Edward of both his wife and home. The question of whether this was his intention doesn't come into the picture. Just as *The Birthday Party* refused to concern itself with whether Stanley's guilt feelings contributed to his undoing, so, in *A Slight Ache,* the matchseller is shown as entirely passive, nothing more than a screen for Edward and Flora to project on. The old man does nothing to set them against each other; what happens is entirely their doing.

On the air, silence is almost tantamount to non-existence – a point that Beckett exploits in his radio plays – and in the broadcast of *A Slight Ache,* the reality of the matchseller was in doubt. Obviously he isn't a fantasy because Edward and Flora both see him and speak to him and Flora feels him, but far from having a clear physical appearance, he seems to Edward to change shape and size,* sometimes to look bigger, like a bullock, sometimes strong, sometimes weak, and to Flora sometimes repulsive, sometimes attractive. In the television production (BBC-2, February 1967, directed by Christopher Morahan) the matchseller was effective so long as the camera was behind him but the close-ups of the one-eyed actor's face all jarred. His non-reaction is far better left to a face we can't see, or can't see clearly.

Edward and Flora both belong to a higher social class than any

* This is rather like the way Mr Knott's appearance keeps changing in Beckett's *Watt.*

of Pinter's earlier characters. They both take considerable pride in their activities, she in her garden, he in his writing, and with both of them, Pinter picks on the right significant details to make the social setting real – the canopy that Flora puts up in the garden for Edward to write under, the polo-shorts, the convolvulus and the honeysuckle, and the gong sounded before meals. All these details are established by references to them – except in the television version, nothing of them is seen or heard by the audience. (For a radio play it has astonishingly few sound effects.) The pride and social superiority of Edward and Flora are necessary to make their humiliation all the greater as they are broken down by the 'harmless old man', although Edward's way of talking is made to sound slightly ridiculous right from the beginning. As the old man's silence drives him into more and more desperate straits in keeping up a one-sided conversation, we hear the anxiety behind the attempt to impress. The clichés clash against the strenuous efforts to present himself as an original and the facts come to sound very much like fiction.

> Yes, I . . . I was in much the same position myself then as you are now, you understand. Struggling to make my way in the world. I was in commerce too. (*With a chuckle.*) Oh, yes, I know what it's like – the weather, the rain, beaten from pillar to post, up hill and down dale . . . the rewards were few . . . winters in hovels . . . up till all hours working at your thesis . . . yes, I've done it all. Let me advise you. Get a good woman to stick by you. Never mind what the world says. Keep at it. Keep your shoulder to the wheel. It'll pay dividends.

In his second scene with the old man Edward gives away so much of himself that there is no chance left of holding on to any kind of pride. From thinking the old man is laughing at him, he sees that he's crying.

> You're weeping. You're shaking with grief. For me. I can't believe it. For my plight. I've been wrong.

Which leads him on to give away still more of himself, until he realizes, with horror, that the man is actually laughing.*

* All this works far better if the uncertainty is entirely Edward's. If we see the man's face, it is ours too.

Harold Pinter

The one element in Edward's humiliation which does not quite fall into place is the mysterious 'slight ache' of the title. It seems to be something that affects his vision although he denies that he has any difficulty in seeing and refuses to let Flora bathe his eyes. But he starts sneezing in his second scene with the matchseller.

> Ah. Fever. Excuse me. (*He blows his nose.*) I've caught a cold. A germ. In my eyes. It was this morning. In my eyes. My eyes. (*Pause. He falls to the floor.*)

Apart from this, his confessions are well written and in the production at the Arts, Emlyn Williams made his self-inflicted downfall very effective.

The changes in Flora are less convincing. Pinter has less sympathy for her and uses her scenes with the matchseller to indulge his predilection for spotting the tart in the lady. In Edward's scenes, we see exactly how each step leads to the next. In Flora's, Pinter shows no real interest in what takes her from contempt to desire. Or, perhaps what interests him is the fact that there is nothing there to cause the transition.

> Really, I think you'd amuse me if you weren't so hideous. You're probably quite amusing in your own way. (*Seductively.*) Tell me all about love. Speak to me of love. (*Pause.*) God knows what you're saying at this very moment. It's quite disgusting. Do you know when I was a girl I loved . . . I loved . . . I simply adored . . . what *have* you got on, for goodness sake? A jersey? It's clogged. Have you been rolling in mud? (*Slight pause.*) You haven't been rolling in mud, have you? (*She rises and goes over to him.*) And what have you got under your jersey? Let's see. (*Slight pause.*) I'm not tickling you, am I? No. Good . . . Lord, is this a vest? That's quite original. Quite original. (*She sits on the arms of his chair.*) Hmmnn, you're solid old boy, I must say. Not at all like a jelly. All you need is a bath. A lovely lathery bath. And a good scrub. A lovely lathery scrub. (*Pause.*) Don't you? It will be a pleasure. (*She throws her arms round him.*) I'm going to keep you.

In the way that affection suddenly emerges, like a threat, this is very much like Ruth's surprise declaration to Lenny in *The Homecoming*.

If you take the glass . . . I'll take you.

In both cases, the surprise is something of a strain on the credulity. It's easy to believe that both women are capable of betraying their men but it's hard to believe in it as happening in the way Pinter makes it happen. The endings of *The Room, The Dumb Waiter, The Birthday Party* and *A Night Out* all have an absolute rightness. They're perfectly consistent with the illogical logic of the play. But to make Flora leave Edward with the matchseller's tray is straining too hard to contrive a neat pattern. In the television production – no doubt with Pinter's approval, since it couldn't have been done without – this ending was cut and the play ended with Edward prostrate on the floor and the matchseller stepping over him as Flora was about to show him over the house, *his* house, she now calls it.

The other element in the play which is unsatisfying is the relationship between the protracted wasp-killing episode at the beginning and the matchseller episode that takes up the rest of the action. It may be that no relationship is intended, but that doesn't mean that no relationship is necessary. Or it may be that a contrast is intended between the reaction of Edward and Flora to the wasp, which they destroy because it frightens them, and to the matchseller, whom they see as a 'harmless old man'. The wasp-killing is theatrically quite effective in itself and useful in establishing Flora and Edward, but the relationship of the two parts of the play to each other and to the 'slight ache' remains unsatisfactory.

A NIGHT OUT

A Night Out, Pinter's next play, which was broadcast in March 1960 and televised a month later, moves about freely from one location to another. This time the immature hero rebels against his dominating mother by making two attempts in one evening to escape from the comforts and the safety of home life. Both times he fails and returns.

The play begins in the same way as *The Birthday Party,* with the woman calling the man's name and the man not answering. As always, the loquacious motherly fussing produces evasiveness in the male.

> MOTHER: Albert, I've been calling you. (*She watches him.*) What are you doing?
> ALBERT: Nothing.
> MOTHER: Didn't you hear me call you, Albert? I've been calling you from upstairs.
> ALBERT: You seen my tie?
> MOTHER: Oh, I say, I'll have to put the flag out.
> ALBERT: What do you mean?
> MOTHER: Cleaning your shoes, Albert? I'll have to put the flag out, won't I?

Albert is twenty-eight but behaves as though he's much younger, putting up with a mother who tries to use him one-sidedly in a relationship which is determined entirely by her needs.

> MOTHER: You promise?
> ALBERT: Promise what?
> MOTHER: That . . . that you won't upset your father.
> ALBERT: My father? How can I upset my father? You're always talking about upsetting people who are dead!
> MOTHER: Oh, Albert, you don't know how you hurt me, you don't know the hurtful way you've got, speaking of your poor father like that.

As a character, though, she doesn't come off as well as Meg. Pinter

32

Paul Rogers as MAX in the Aldwych production of *The Homecoming*.

Derek Godfrey as LAW, Kika Markham as JANE, and Harold Pinter as STOTT in *The Basement* on BBC Television.

tends to be better when writing about mother-substitutes rather than actual mothers. His best mother-substitute of all is the father in the all-male household in *The Homecoming.*

The second scene in *A Night Out* is at a coffee-stall, and, as in *The Dumb Waiter,* Pinter enjoys himself with a conversation about football, writing this time from the viewpoint of the players. Albert, we soon gather, has let the side down.

> KEDGE: He's a good ball-player, that Connor, isn't he?
>
> SEELEY: Look. I said Albert before the kick-off, Connor's on the right wing, I said, play your normal game. I told him six times before the kick-off.
>
> KEDGE: What's the good of him playing his normal game? He's a left half, he's not a left back.
>
> SEELEY: Yes, but he's a defensive left half, isn't he? That's why I told him to play his normal game. You don't want to worry about Connor, I said, he's a good ball-player but he's not all that good.
>
> KEDGE: Oh, he's good, though.
>
> SEELEY: No one's denying he's good. But he's not all that good. I mean, he's not tip-top. You know what I mean?
>
> KEDGE: He's fast.
>
> SEELEY: He's fast, but he's not all that fast, is he?
>
> KEDGE (*doubtfully*): Well, not all that fast . . .

Albert arrives late, having had difficulty in getting away from the mother, who's been trying to make herself indispensable to him and delaying his departure by insisting on brushing his suit, straightening his tie and giving him a clean handkerchief for his breast pocket. When he finally appears, Albert shows himself to be insecure about girls, not really keen, after all, to go to the party, and very nettled when one of the boys inquires maliciously about his mother's health. This prepares us for the outbreak of violence at the party. The others all resent Albert because he's so quiet, and he's baited by the boys, led on by the girls and finally blamed for an incident when one of the girls screams. In fact it is the old man in whose honour the party is being given who touches her. Again as in *The Birthday Party,* the fighting is started by the least aggressive character on stage. The weapon of the aggressor is words and the physical violence

Harold Pinter

comes only when the victim breaks. The line that makes Albert hit out at the ringleader of his enemies is 'You're a mother's boy'.*

Returning home, Albert is at once the object of another bullying verbal attack from his mother. She accuses him of 'mucking about with girls', complains about the state of his clothes, refuses to believe he's been at the firm's party, informs him that he hasn't eaten anything all evening so he must have his dinner, reproaches him for not bringing home a really nice girl and introducing her, remonstrates about the high hopes his father had for him and praises herself for keeping such a lovely home, but her chief complaint is:

> Not for years, not for years, have you come up to me and said, Mum, I love you, like you did when you were a little boy. You've never said it without me having to ask you. Not since before your father died.

Again Albert is provoked into aggression. He seizes the clock from the table and raises it above his head to hit her. And again he goes out.

But the tart who picks him up turns out to be just as fussy and irritating as the mother. She's one of Pinter's essays in lower-class snobbery, and he holds the balance very well between what is virtually a monologue from her and Albert's one-word reactions. The tart talks proudly about the aristocratic features of the little girl in the photograph on the mantelpiece, saying it's her daughter, although actually it's herself when young. She lies about the smart boarding school the little girl is at, complains that the neighbourhood is 'full of people of no class at all', and doesn't allow Albert to swear, to sit in her chair or to drop ash on the carpet. She even attacks the morality of other girls, though she's curious to know how far they go. Again, the meek man is provoked into violence, dropping a lighted cigarette on her carpet and using force to keep her away when she goes to pick it up. Albert is now the dangerous intruder in somebody else's room. Terrorizing her into silence by threatening her with the clock, he revenges himself for her monologue by having one of his own,

* In the second television production, directed by Christopher Morahan on BBC 2 in February 1967, Albert punches Seeley by mistake and apologizes to him.

34

in which, incoherently, all his grievances about his mother and about the party come out in one long stream of protest.

> ALBERT: You're all the same, you see, you're all the same, you're just a dead weight round my neck. What makes you think... What makes you think you can... tell me... It's the same as this business about the light in Grandma's room. Always something. Always something. (*To her.*) My ash? I'll put it where I like! You see this clock? Watch your step. Just watch your step.
>
> GIRL: Stop this. What are you —?
>
> ALBERT (*seizing her wrist, with trembling, controlled violence*): Watch your step! (*Stammering.*) I've had – I've had – I've had – just about enough. Get it?... You know what I did?... I'm just telling you, that's all. (*Breathlessly.*) You haven't got any breeding. She hadn't either. And what about those girls tonight? Same kind. And that one. I didn't touch her!

Once he's made her knuckle under to his will-power, he celebrates in the same way as Wally does with the girl in *Night School* – by giving her orders. He makes her walk to the wall, cover her face, pick her shoes up, put them on. Like Wally and Stanley he doesn't know what he wants from the girl and he leaves without sleeping with her. He goes home to find his mother offended but unhurt. In fact he hadn't hit her: the impression we got that he had was a piece of cheating, easy to bring off on radio and television* but harder to bring off on stage. The ultimate humiliation for Albert and the ultimate sign of the lack of contact between them is the mother's forgiveness.

> Listen, Albert, I'll tell you what I'm going to do. I'm going to forget all about it... We'll have your holiday in a fortnight. We can go away. (*She strokes his hand.*) We'll go away ... together.

---

* Christopher Morahan's production didn't attempt to give the impression that Albert hit his mother. We saw his arm frozen in the air with the clock raised threateningly but it was obvious the threat wouldn't be carried out before the picture faded. This took a lot of the force out of Albert's 'You know what I did?' in the scene with the tart and a lot of the tension out of the whole scene, because we no longer thought of Albert as having come out of the house because his mother was lying there unconscious.

THE CARETAKER

The Caretaker is an easier play to 'understand' than *The Birthday Party*, though not without its mystifications and its obscurities, and the London production boasted a brilliant performance by Donald Pleasence, which helped to make it a commercial success. But what helped still more was the fact that Pinter's name was very much in fashion by then.

Not that the play didn't deserve its long run. Within its limits – and basically it's only a one-act play teased out into a more usable length – it's often very funny, very effective and even moving. As a character, Davies comes off as well in the writing as he did in Pleasence's performance, but Pinter doesn't achieve anything like the same success with either of the brothers. Aston comes off better than Mick, partly because the room is an extension of his personality. He's compulsive about accumulating objects from junk shops – cupboards, boxes, vases, drawers, tools, ornaments, chairs and all the assorted lumber that gives the room its special atmosphere. It is also, one gathers, the same feeling that 'this might come in useful one day' which makes him pick up Davies. The compulsiveness, the vague goodwill, the hours-long lingering over petty household jobs like putting a plug on the toaster, the fumbling friendship with Davies, and the good intentions that will never take effect are all sketched in effectively.

Where the characterization fails is in its departure from Pinter's normal practice. Aston's long narrative speech at the end of Act Two, describing the episode in the mental hospital, has been highly praised by some critics but it gives us information we don't need and clashes badly with the style of the writing all round it. While Davies's speeches about his past may be fact or fiction or a mixture of the two, and while Mick's speeches are mostly fiction, Aston is giving us something that we are obviously meant to swallow whole. Worst of all, it comes across as oddly old-fashioned. Pinter knows as well as anyone how unnecessary it is to explain present behaviour in terms of past history, but here he's doing just that.

But the partial failure with Aston is less serious than the failure with Mick, who is very effective when silent but often disastrous when he speaks. He provides an air of mystery and tension at the very beginning of the play by appearing and then going out when he hears the voices of the others approaching. He also provides all the violence and the suspense of the moments when he's terrorizing Davies or goading him into drawing his knife. He plays practical tricks on him in the dark, effectively enough, but the blackout he produces is nothing like so frightening as its prototype in *The Birthday Party*. It comes at the beginning of one of the many short scenes in the play. Davies comes in, tries the light switch and can't make it work. He moves about, stumbling. He lights a match but it goes out and he drops the box, which is kicked away. He gets scared and from talking to himself he starts shouting to the invisible intruder that he's got a knife. He stumbles, falls, cries out and whimpers. Then in the silence, Mick starts the Electrolux, moving the nozzle along the floor. Davies skips away terrified and flattens himself against the wall, knife in hand. Switching the light on, Mick announces laconically that he was just doing some spring cleaning.

Episodes like this come off in exactly the way Pinter wants them to, but Mick's long speeches don't.

> You remind me of my uncle's brother. He was always on the move, that man. Never without his passport. Had an eye for the girls. Very much your build. Bit of an athlete. Long-jump specialist. He had a habit of demonstrating different run-ups in the drawing-room round about Christmas-time. Had a penchant for nuts. That's what it was. Nothing else but a penchant. Couldn't eat enough of them. Peanuts, walnuts, brazil nuts, monkey nuts, wouldn't touch a piece of fruit cake. Had a marvellous stop-watch. Picked it up in Hong Kong. The day after they chucked him out of the Salvation Army. Used to go in number four for Beckenham Reserves. That was before he got his Gold Medal. Had a funny habit of carrying his fiddle on his back. Like a papoose. I think there was a bit of the Red Indian in him. To be honest, I've never made out how he came to be my uncle's brother. I've often thought that maybe it was the other way round. I mean that my uncle was his brother and he was my uncle. But I never called him uncle. As a matter of fact I called him Sid. My

mother called him Sid too. It was a funny business. Your spitting image he was. Married a Chinaman and went to Jamaica.

The gratuitous reminiscing about relations is rather like Goldberg's, but the surreal touches look forward to *The Collection* and *The Homecoming*. But coming so soon after the violence that ended Act One – the action is continuous – the speech destroys a lot of the tension with its funny but free-wheeling irrelevancies. Mick's reactions to Davies are almost as confusing to us as they are to the old man. Basically it's clear that he's jealous of his brother's relationship with him and that he wants to get rid of him. But he goes to the most improbable lengths in order to do this. He alternates between scaring him and trying to make friends with him, so as to woo him away from Aston. He succeeds in getting Davies to come to him with complaints about his brother. That Mick should then turn against Davies is predictable and doesn't make any useful point. Altogether, the treatment of Mick seems to suffer from a lack of interest in him except as a means of producing mystification and stage terror.

Davies is a very much more successful creation. Pinter obviously shares Beckett's interest in tramps and he does very well with the two female tramps in *The Black and White*. Davies is the most fully-rounded character in Pinter, and the characterization doesn't depend at all on giving us any information about Davies's past. We gather that he's spent much of his life on the road and that he's just been working in the kitchen of a café, but otherwise we learn all we need to know about him through what he says and above all through what he leaves unsaid. His evasiveness is given a rhythm in the dialogue which Pleasence caught superbly in the performance.

> DAVIES: There's a caff down there, you see, might be able to get fixed up there. I was there, see? I know they were a bit short-handed. They might be in the need of a bit of staff.
> ASTON: When was that?
> DAVIES: Eh? Oh, well, that was . . . near on . . . that'll be . . . that'll be a little while ago now. But of course what it is, they can't find the right kind of people in these places. What they want to do, they're trying to do away with these foreigners,

you see, in catering. I mean, that's what they're aiming at.
That's one thing I know for a fact.

ASTON: Hmmn.

DAVIES: See, I was thinking, once I got down there, I might have
a look in at the stadium, at Wembley Stadium. For all the big
matches, get my meaning? They need people down there to
run the ground, see, to keep the ground. Or another thing I
could do, I could go along down there to Kennington Oval. All
these big sports grounds, it stands to reason, they need people,
to keep the ground, that's what they want, that's what they're
crying out for. It's only common sense, en't? Oh, I got all that
under way ... that's ... uh ... that's ... what I'll be doing.

A lifetime of procrastination is audible not only in the phrases but
in the way they're joined together. But, like the tart in *A Night Out,*
Davies is a great snob: 'I've eaten dinner off the best of plates.' He
considers himself superior to the Indians who live next door and
tries to blame them for the noises he's been making in his sleep. 'I
tell you what, maybe it were them Blacks.' He claims to have left his
wife because he found her dirty underwear in the vegetable pan and
he feels superior to Aston – at least *he's* never been in a mental
hospital. Pinter extracts every ounce of comedy from Davies's
incongruous vanities.

Once again there's a great deal of emphasis on the room and some
mystery about who the landlord is. When Davies tries to find out,
Aston is evasive, but implies that the house belongs to him. Mick
later insists that it's his. And again, the script is very vague about the
other rooms in the house. 'They're out of commission,' we are told.
Nor do we ever find out where Mick sleeps now. But like Wally in
Night School, he seems to be possessed by immature jealousy because someone else has been given the bed that used to be his, and
he seems to be nervous of the old man in some way, although Davies,
apart from his smell, is obviously just as innocuous as the matchseller was in *A Slight Ache.*

The other major success of the play is in exploring and comparing
and making so much capital out of the fantasies of two such off-beat
characters as Davies and Aston, and in linking them together into
the context of the room. The collection of junk in the background is

there all the time as an ironic visual counterpoint to everything Aston says about his plans for the house. We know that the things he thought would come in useful never will, we know that he'll never mend the plug or build the shed or put up the partition.

> Once I get that shed up outside . . . I'll be able to give a bit more thought to the flat, you see. Perhaps I can knock up one or two things for it. (*He walks to the window.*) I can work with my hands, you see. That's one thing I can do. I never knew I could. But I can do all sorts of things now, with my hands. You know, manual things. When I get that shed up out there . . . I'll have a workshop, you see. I . . . could do a bit of woodwork. Simple woodwork, to start. Working with . . . good wood.
> (*Pause.*)
> Of course, there's a lot to be done to this place. What I think, though, I think I'll put in a partition . . . in one of the rooms along the landing. I think it'll take it. You know . . . they've got these screens . . . you know . . . Oriental. They break up a room with them. Make it into two parts. I could either do that or I could have a partition. I could knock them up, you see, if I had a workshop.
> (*Pause.*)
> Anyway, I think I've decided on the partition.

Aston's manner of speaking is quite adequately differentiated from Davies's, but there's something of the same rhythm of procrastination in both. The scenes between the two of them contain some of the vaguest dialogue that's ever been written, but it's precise enough in making its point about the speakers.

> DAVIES: . . . I never been a caretaker before.
> (*Pause.*)
> ASTON: How do you feel about being one, then?
> DAVIES: Well, I reckon . . . Well, I'd have to know . . . you know . . .
> ASTON: What sort of . . .
> DAVIES: Yes, what sort of . . . you know . . .
> (*Pause.*)
> ASTON: Well, I mean . . .
> DAVIES: I mean, I'd have to . . . I'd have to . . .
> ASTON: Well, I could tell you . . .

DAVIES: That's . . . that's it . . . you see . . . you get my meaning?

ASTON: When the time comes . . .

DAVIES: I mean, that's what I'm getting at, you see . . .

ASTON: More or less exactly what you . . .

DAVIES: You see, what I mean to say . . . what I'm getting at is . . . I mean, what sort of jobs . . .

(*Pause.*)

ASTON: Well, there's things like the stairs . . . and the . . . the bells . . .

DAVIES: But it'd be a matter . . . wouldn't it . . . it'd be a matter of a broom . . . isn't it?

ASTON: You could have a duster . . .

DAVIES: Oh, I know I could have that . . . but I couldn't manage without a . . . without a broom . . . could I?

ASTON: You'd have to have a broom . . .

DAVIES: That's it . . . that's just what I was thinking . . .

ASTON: I'd be able to pick one up for you, without much trouble . . . and of course, you'd . . . need a few brushes . . .

DAVIES: You'd need implements . .   you see . . . you'd need a good few implements . . .

They're like two children, delighted at finding uses for the words they've picked up, but not really believing in the plans that they're making for the objects they've picked up. Somewhere, they know it's all a game. Pinter makes this clear without losing his sympathy for them.

If it had been a one-act play, centred on making this point and the immediately relevant points, *The Caretaker* might have come off brilliantly. As it is, it's thin in places and padded out in others. The conversation about different kinds of saws, for instance, goes on too long, and some of the blackout lines are weak, repeating notes that have been struck already, instead of striking new ones. After writing so much for television, Pinter obviously found it easier to go on working in short scenes, but the discontinuity is sometimes distracting.

The failure with Mick is a curious one. He doesn't belong to the play in the same way that Aston and Davies do and his fantasies, whatever they are, are not subject to the same scrutiny. His enjoyment of teasing Davies is obvious enough and it's quite effective and rather pathetic when Davies falls so readily into the trap of complaining to him about Aston. After this, the end is predictable and inevitable. Davies has tried to join forces with his enemy against the man who has befriended him. In any case, he is the intruder in the room and he has to be thrown out. The parting between Aston and Davies at the end of the play has an odd kind of poignancy. But it doesn't leave us, as the end of *The Birthday Party* did, with a sense of solid experience behind us.

NIGHT SCHOOL

Night School is another play which started its life on the radio before being translated to television. This time the mother role is divided between two aunts, Annie and Milly. They've betrayed their nephew Wally by letting his room to a girl while he was serving a prison sentence, so that a struggle for possession of the room ensues on his return. He's offended to find that the girl has made his room effeminate.

> Look at those frills. Frills . . . all over the place. Bloody dolls' house. My damn room.

But he's not man enough to seize the chance of making a take-over bid for the room with her in it. Instead of letting her see him for what he really is, a very petty criminal, he puts on a hopeless act of being big. And instead of reacting to the real girl in front of him, he goes for help to a father-figure (the landlord) asking him to locate a girl from a photograph, without realizing that it's the same girl.

It's a neat idea for a plot – a bit like *A Slight Ache*, perhaps, in being rather too patterned, and once again you only have to scratch the nice girl to find the tart underneath. Sally is made to behave so differently with the aunts from the way she behaves in the club that she's hardly the same person. But a lot of the dialogue is very good and Pinter has a great deal of fun on the way with names (Milly, Sally, Wally, Tully), and with rhymes (Lascar from Madagascar). What's more important, though, is that he's developing the technique of the bravura boasting fantasy, putting in some very bizarre touches that look forward to both Harry and Bill in *The Collection* and to Lenny in *The Homecoming*. Walter's fantasies are very much more elaborate than Albert's lies to the tart in *A Night Out* about being an Assistant Director in films.

> WALTER: Ever met a gunman before?
> SALLY: I don't think so.
> WALTER: It's not a bad life, all things considered. Plenty of time off. You know, holidays with pay, you could say. No there's

Harold Pinter

plenty of worse occupations. You're not frightened of me now you know I'm a gunman, are you?

SALLY: No, I think you're charming.

WALTER: Oh, you're right there. That's why I got on so well in prison, you see. Charm. You know what I was doing in there, I was running the prison library. I was the best librarian they ever had. The day I left the Governor gave me a personal send off. Saw me all the way to the gate. He told me business at the library had shot up out of all recognition since I'd been in charge.

SALLY: What a wonderful compliment.

WALTER (*pouring more drink*): He told me that if I'd consider giving up armed robbery he'd recommend me for a job in the British Museum. Looking after rare manuscripts. You know, writing my opinion of them.

SALLY: I should think that's quite a skilled job.

WALTER: Cheers. Skilled? Well, funny enough, I've had a good bit to do with rare manuscripts in my time. I used to know a bloke who ran a business digging them up.

SALLY: Digging what up?

WALTER: Rare manuscripts. Out of tombs. I used to give him a helping hand when I was on the loose. Very well paid it was too. You see, they were nearly always attached to a corpse, these manuscripts, you had to lift up the pelvis bone with a pair of tweezers. Big tweezers. Can't leave finger-prints on a corpse, you see. Canon law. The biggest shock I ever had was when a skeleton collapsed on top of me and nearly bit my ear off. I had a funny feeling at that moment. I thought I was the skeleton and he was my long lost uncle come to kiss me goodnight. You've never been inside a grave, I suppose. I can recommend it, honest, I mean if you want to taste everything life has to offer.

Solto, the landlord, is a kind of Goldberg, but he makes less impact and isn't so funny. He talks at length about himself in much the same way, with Jewish rhythms clearly discernible in his speech. He also repeats the Goldberg pattern of wooing the girl away from the young man (towards whom he pretends to be well-disposed) and taking her for himself.

While the night-club dialogue is typical of Pinter, with its repetitiveness and its definite rhythm, it's also very reminiscent of the T. S. Eliot of *Sweeney Agonistes*.

DUSTY: How about Pereira?
DORIS: What about Pereira?
            I don't care.
DUSTY: You don't care!
            Who pays the rent?
DORIS: Yes he pays the rent.
DUSTY: Well some men don't and some men do.
            Some men don't and you know who.
DORIS: You can have Pereira.

TULLY: . . . Don't you remember me at Blackheath.
SOLTO: You're going back a bit.
TULLY: I'm going back a few years before the war.
SOLTO: You're going back to when the game was good.
TULLY: What about you at Blackheath?
SOLTO: Blackheath. It's another story when you start talking about Blackheath.

Perhaps Pinter owes more to T. S. Eliot than has been recognized.

THE DWARFS

The Dwarfs, which was staged at the Arts in December 1960, is
hardly a play at all. Taken from Pinter's unpublished novel of the
same name, it's a completely unstructured series of fragmentary and
often incoherent conversations between three friends, Len, Pete and
Mark. The main interest of the piece is that it shows us in their crudest
form some of the themes which Pinter developed in the plays.

It starts off with a scene where Len and Pete are eating and drinking
in Mark's room, complaining, like the gunmen in *The Dumb Waiter,*
that so little has been laid on for them. A lot of the dialogue is
schizophrenic, and not put into sufficient perspective by Pete's
telling Len that he's heading for the looney bin or by Len's telling
Pete that he's a nut. Often the rhythm is so strong that it verges
on verse and one of Len's speeches is laid out like verse. Again
language and some of the cadences make us think of T. S. Eliot.

MARK: What do you think of it?
LEN: It's not a schmutta.
MARK: It's got a zip at the hips.
LEN: A zip at the hips? What for?
MARK: Instead of a buckle. It's neat.
LEN: Neat? I should say it's neat.
MARK: No turn-ups.
LEN: I can see that. Why didn't you have turn-ups?
MARK: It's smarter without turn-ups.
LEN: Of course it's smarter without turn-ups.
MARK: I didn't want it double-breasted.
LEN: Double-breasted? Of course you couldn't have it double-
breasted.
MARK: What do you think of the cloth?
LEN: The cloth? (*He examines it, gasps and whistles through his
teeth. At a great pace.*) What a piece of cloth. What a piece of
cloth. What a piece of cloth. What a piece of cloth. What a
piece of *cloth.*
MARK: You like the cloth?
LEN: WHAT A PIECE OF CLOTH!

(It may also have been T. S. Eliot who infected Pinter with the delight he takes in the names of London districts.)

The action moves from Mark's room to Len's room and for Len, his room isn't the safe and stable place that a room usually is.

> The rooms we live in . . . open and shut. (*Pause.*) Can't you see? They change shape at their own will. I wouldn't grumble if only they would keep to some consistency. But they don't. And I can't tell the limits, the boundaries, which I've been led to believe are natural. I'm all for the natural behaviour of rooms, doors, staircases, the lot. But I can't rely on them.

Pete has one very explicit speech which starts off rather like the speech of Teddy's which I quoted from *The Homecoming*.

> The apprehension of experience must obviously be dependent upon discrimination if it's to be considered valuable. That's what you lack. You've got no idea how to preserve a distance between what you smell and what you think about it. You haven't got the faculty for making a simple distinction between one thing and another.

But it veers off into a description of a dream of being trapped on a platform in a tube station and seeing people's faces disintegrating, lumps of flesh falling off. The image of the mirror and the fear of losing identity are recurrent motifs and there seems to be a connection between these and the image of the scavenger dwarfs of the title, who seem to feed on people, as Pete and Len were trying to feed off Mark's supplies in his absence. But none of this is at all clear. We're told that the dwarfs only work in cities and the way Len speaks of their being 'on the job' makes us associate them with Goldberg and McCann or Gus and Ben.

The script becomes more and more incoherent as it goes on. Len feels used, persecuted by the other two, talks of the hole they've made in his side, which he can't plug. The writing becomes surreal, Joycean, mad, and the madness is blamed on to the food. Len says he's eaten too much stale cheese – 'It got me in the end' – and then suddenly the language becomes very clear again as Len makes an explicit statement about the nature of identity.

Harold Pinter

The point is, who are you? Not why or how, not even what. I can see what, perhaps, clearly enough. But who are you? It's no use saying you know who you are just because you tell me you can fit your particular key into a particular slot which will only receive your particular key because that's not foolproof and certainly not conclusive. Just because you're inclined to make these statements of faith has nothing to do with me. It's not my business. Occasionally I believe I perceive a little of what you are but that's pure accident. Pure accident on both our parts, the perceived and the perceiver. It's nothing like an accident, it's deliberate, it's a joint pretence. We depend on these accidents, on these contrived accidents, to continue. It's not important then that it's conspiracy or hallucination. What you are, or appear to be to me, or appear to be to you, changes so quickly, so horrifyingly, I certainly can't keep up with it and I'm damn sure you can't either. But who you are I can't even begin to recognize, and sometimes I recognize it so wholly, so forcibly, I can't look, and how can I be certain of what I see? You have no number. Where am I to look, where am I to look, what is there to locate, so as to have some surety, to have some rest from this whole bloody racket? You're the sum of so many reflections. How many reflections? Whose reflections? Is that what you consist of? What scum does the tide leave? What happens to the scum? When does it happen? I've seen what happens. But I can't speak when I see it. I can only point a finger. I can't even do that. The scum is broken and sucked back. I don't see where it goes, I don't see when, what do I see, what have I seen? What have I seen, the scum or the essence? What about it? Does all this give you the right to stand there and tell me you know who you are? It's a bloody impertinence.

THE COLLECTION

The Collection was first seen on television in May 1961 and staged at the Aldwych in June 1962, jointly directed by Peter Hall and Harold Pinter. It's written in short scenes which are put together extremely well and its dialogue is full of thrust and bite, though the stage production didn't make the impact it could have made, in spite of a nicely judged performance from Michael Hordern as Harry.

Compared with the rest of Pinter's later work, *The Collection* is remarkable for its economy. There's no padding and all the details count. The fruit juice, the olives and Stella's kitten all contribute, not to the plot, but to the characterization and atmosphere, which are built up subtly, without explicitness. As usual in Pinter, we learn next to nothing about the surrounding circumstances. All four characters are involved in the dress business, but Pinter only mentions this in passing. And of course we learn nothing about motivation. Why is James so intent on making some kind of personal contact with Bill? What does Stella feel towards each of the three men? The four characters are linked together by emotional interdependencies but there's no question of sorting out the tangle of crossed lines. What Pinter gives us has to be enough and, in its curious way, it is. The play stands up as a satisfying whole, even though we are given so few facts and even though so much of what the characters themselves say may be fiction. Perhaps Harry's story about picking Bill up in an East End slum is true. Perhaps it's a distortion of the truth. Perhaps it's a complete fiction. Where Pinter succeeds so well is in establishing a convention and a frame of plot development in which the unanswered questions don't distract us from looking at what he wants to show us or prevent us from being satisfied with what he gives us. The value of the incident in Leeds, whatever it was, is that its consequences illuminate all the insecurities that the characters have about themselves and about each other. Harry doesn't trust Bill, James doesn't trust Stella, and neither Bill nor Stella, obviously, are finding fulfilment in their lives

Harold Pinter

with their partners. Without sketching in any of the past history of these relationships or even developing them very much in the present tense, Pinter draws on the insecurities to build up a most effective tension.

This time we have two rooms and two couples, with one member of each couple as a threat to the peace of the other couple. The play starts very much like a conventional thriller with a dim figure inside a telephone box at four o'clock in the morning. Inside Harry's house, the ringing of the telephone announces the menace from outside. We then find from the way he talks to Harry that Bill is apprehensive about meeting the stranger who is so persistent in trying to contact him. But once the two men meet, although the tension survives, the tenor of the conversation is very different from that of the conventional husband talking to the man he suspects of having slept with his wife.

> JAMES: Got any olives?
> BILL: How did you know my name?
> JAMES: No olives?
> BILL: Olives? I'm afraid not.
> JAMES: You mean to say you don't keep olives for your guests?
> BILL: You're not my guest, you're an intruder. What can I do for you?
> JAMES: Do you mind if I sit down?
> BILL: Yes, I do.
> JAMES: You'll get over it.
> (*James sits. Bill stands. James stands, takes off his overcoat, throws it on an armchair, and sits again.*)
> BILL: What's your name, old boy?
> (*James reaches to a bowl of fruit and breaks off a grape, which he eats.*)
> JAMES: Where shall I put the pips?
> BILL: In your wallet.
> (*James takes out his wallet and deposits the pips.*)

The conversation which follows contains some good examples of Pinter's developing technique for suggesting tension beneath a surface of apparent relaxation. And once again, as in *Night School*, Bill's outrageous boasts also point to his insecurity.

BILL: I'm expecting guests in a minute, you know. Cocktails, I'm standing for Parliament next season.
JAMES: Come here.
BILL: I'm going to be Minister for Home Affairs.

But quite apart from the comedy and the fantasy, the conversation is well developed on serious lines as the characters take up positions in relation to the mystery of what really happened. James speaks as if his wife has given him a full confession of how she met Bill in the lift, how he went to her room in pyjamas and dressing-gown, asking for toothpaste, and how he refused to leave. As for us, we have no means of knowing whether his wife was telling the truth or whether he's telling Bill the truth about what his wife said to him. We know that Bill was in Leeds and we know that James knew Bill's name, but that's all. Bill's reactions are inconsistent, varying between amused dismissals of the charge and indications that he did sleep with the woman. But again we have no means of knowing whether the inconsistency is deliberate, contrived in order to tantalize James, or not. The scene is something like the party scene in *The Birthday Party*: we have the hunter and the hunted; we have the conflict going on under the small-talk as the characters drink; we have the mystery that adds to the menace – we don't know quite what it's all about. But the violence and the comedy are much more closely interwoven now.

BILL: . . . Ah well, it's been very nice meeting you, old chap. You must come again when the weather's better.
(*James makes a sudden move forward. Bill starts back, and falls over a pouffe on to the floor James chuckles. Pause.*)
You've made me spill my drink. You've made me spill it on my cardigan.
(*James stands over him.*)
I could easily kick you from here.
(*Pause.*)

Harry is the character who is least directly involved in the question but he too is jealous and this makes him behave just as erratically as the jealous James or the evasive Bill. Pinter writes mad fantasy speeches for him with elaborate casualness.

Harold Pinter

> BILL: I don't want any potatoes, thank you.
> HARRY: No potatoes? What an extraordinary thing. Yes, this chap, he was asking for you, he wanted you.
> BILL: What for?
> HARRY: He wanted to know if you ever cleaned your shoes with furniture polish.
> BILL: Really? How odd.
> HARRY: Not odd. Some kind of national survey.
> BILL: What did he look like?
> HARRY: Oh . . . lemon hair, nigger-brown teeth, wooden leg, bottle-green eyes and a toupee. Know him?

But side by side with the embroidery and the amusement, the edge and the incisiveness of the dialogue are never lost.

Back with Stella, James taunts her by appearing to be debating with himself about whether or not to do what we know he's done already – to go to see Bill. When he finally admits that he's seen him, he describes, comically, a dinner with him, which probably he never had. Or if he did have it, it wasn't at all like this. But again we're forced into playing the game of guessing how much of what he says is fiction.

> JAMES: . . . He entirely confirmed your story.
> STELLA: Did he?
> JAMES: Mmm. Only thing – he rather implied that you led him on. Typical masculine thing to say, of course.
> STELLA: That's a lie.
> JAMES: You know what men are. I reminded him that you'd resisted, and you'd hated the whole thing, but that you'd been – how can we say – somehow hypnotized by him, it happens sometimes. He agreed it can happen sometimes. He told me he'd been hypnotized once by a cat. Wouldn't go into any more details, though. Still, I must admit we rather hit it off. We've got the same interests. He was most amusing over the brandy.

By now we're involved in such a complex calculus of distortion that we're quite contented to lose sight of the basic question of whether Bill slept with Stella, which must be answerable with a simple yes or no.

Stella is the least satisfactory character. Pinter allows her no humour and no fantasy. Put under pressure, all she can do is burst into tears, and James's long speech about Bill is implicitly a criticism of the limitations of their marriage. It's like Mick in *The Caretaker* talking down to Davies about the chaps he knows, making them sound far more interesting than the person he's talking to.

> He's a very cultivated bloke, your bloke, quite a considerable intelligence at work there, I thought. He's got a collection of Chinese pots stuck on a wall, must have cost at least fifteen hundred a piece. Well, you can't help noticing that sort of thing. I mean, you couldn't say he wasn't a man of taste. He's brimming over with it. Well, I suppose he must have struck you the same way. No, really, I think I should thank you, rather than anything else. After two years of marriage it looks as though, by accident, you've opened up a whole new world for me.

At the end, the conflict is resolved and the pattern completed very neatly, without of course answering the basic question. Harry repeats James's telephone trick by ringing up Stella and not saying who he is. There's a very 'Pinteresque' scene in which violence seems to be pending and James throws a knife at Bill's face, which makes him cut his hand in catching it. But the fact that Harry is standing in the doorway reduces the tension in one way to heighten it in another. It's Harry who finally takes charge of the situation by telling James that Stella has confessed to him that the whole story was made up. But, as before, we know neither whether Stella told Harry the truth nor whether Harry is telling Bill and James the truth about what Stella told him.

In any case the important part of the scene isn't what Harry says about Stella but what he says about Bill. He's given good, terse, humorous, cutting lines all through the scene, culminating in a long speech with many reiterations of the word 'slum'.

> Bill's a slum boy, you see, he's got a slum sense of humour. That's why I never take him along with me to parties. Because he's got a slum mind. I have nothing against slum minds *per se*, you understand, nothing at all. There's a certain kind of slum mind which is perfectly all right in a slum, but when this kind of slum mind gets out of the slum it sometimes persists, you see, it rots everything. That's what Bill is. There's something faintly putrid about him, don't you find? Like a slug. There's nothing wrong

53

with slugs in their place, but he's a slum slug; there's nothing wrong with slum slugs in their place, but this one won't keep his place – he crawls all over the walls of nice houses, leaving slime, don't you, boy? He confirms stupid sordid little stories just to amuse himself, while everyone else has to run round in circles to get to the root of the matter and smooth the whole thing out. All he can do is sit and suck his bloody hand and decompose like the filthy putrid slum slug he is.

After this, Bill tells James what he says is the real truth – that he sat in the lounge with Stella for two hours, talking about what they'd do together if they went up to her room, but never going. James seems to accept this as the truth, since he goes home and confronts Stella with it. She neither confirms nor denies it, and of course Pinter is quite right not to let her.

THE LOVER

The Lover, which was televised in March 1963 and staged six months later, received more publicity than *The Collection,* but it's not such a good play. It's thinner in texture and the idea is dragged out to greater length than it really warrants. It has certain resemblances to *The Collection.* The game that Richard and Sarah play with each other by pretending that they're being unfaithful to each other in the afternoon, when Sarah's afternoon lover is actually Richard in different clothes, isn't altogether unlike the games the characters play in *The Collection* by telling each other lies about the alleged infidelity. And in both cases, part of the tension for us is the game that Pinter's playing in making us try to sort out the fiction from the facts. In both plays, the game has an unpleasant side to it, and the characters work up a good deal of real anger about infidelities which may be imaginary, but the anger illuminates characteristics which wouldn't otherwise have been seen.

As in *The Collection,* we find out very little about the surrounding circumstances. Where Richard's money comes from, whether he really has an office, what he does and where he changes his clothes all remain mysteries. We know nothing about him except the way he talks and behaves in the two roles that he's chosen for himself. As in *The Collection,* the woman's character is less explored than the man's. Sarah varies between yielding and resisting, but it's always Richard who takes the initiative and he's the one who finally gets bored with the game and starts to break its rules, dragging the apparatus of the afternoon (the bongo drums) into the evening and forbidding Stella to go on receiving her lover.

But it's in the development of this change in Richard that we see that the writing is less successful than in *The Collection.* With all the questions that the earlier play left unanswered, we never felt that we wanted more information than it was giving us, and however obscure the characters' motives remained, we never felt that we needed to know more about them. Here, however, it's difficult to accept Richard's change of attitude as necessary to him. It's necessary

55

to the script as being a twist to take the situation further, but as a development of the character as established, it seems contrived.

Again as in *The Collection,* there's a great deal of charm in the writing, particularly in the affectation of smiling casualness when matters are being discussed that normally would make tempers rise.

RICHARD (*amiably*): Is your lover coming today?
SARAH: Mmnn.
RICHARD: What time?
SARAH: Three.
RICHARD: Will you be going out . . . or staying in?
SARAH: Oh . . . I think we'll stay in.
RICHARD: I thought you wanted to go to that exhibition.
SARAH: I did, yes . . . but I think I'd prefer to stay in with him today.
RICHARD: Mmn-hmmn. Well, I must be off.

But the development of the situation lacks the economy we've come to expect of Pinter and as they go on talking to each other about their lovers in several different scenes, separated by fades and quick costume changes, nothing very much is added. A superfluous scene with the milkman has to be written in to give Richard time to change his clothes in order to be Max the lover.*

The silent scene with the bongo drums was more effective on television, where the director, Joan Kemp-Welch, showed us their fingers in close-up, first scratching at each other and at the drum, tapping the drumskin with a build-up of excitement until his fingers pounced on her fingers like a tarantula and with her hand trying frantically to escape, flailing at the drum. And then, after this sexy prologue to it, they play their first game. Richard pretends to be Max pretending to be a stranger accosting her in a park and then to be the kindly park-keeper who rescues her and takes her into his hut.

This scene is very good up to the point where he says 'It's teatime, Mary,' and they both disappear under the tablecloth together, but in the ensuing conversation, Richard (in his role as the lover) discusses with Sarah the attitude of her husband to the knowledge that his

---

* When the play was televised, the critic of one of the daily papers thought it was a false economy to let one actor play the two parts.

wife has a lover. This is too much like the preceding conversation
before we knew that he was the lover and he was discussing exactly
the same question in his role as the husband. The tension increases
slightly when Richard makes Max threaten to get together with
Richard (just like James's threat to Stella in *The Collection)* and to
end the affair. Sarah is displeased at his departure from the normal
routine.

> I want to whisper something to you. Listen. Let me whisper to
> you. Mmmm? Can I? Please? It's whispering time. Earlier it
> was teatime, wasn't it? Wasn't it? Now it's whispering time.
> (*Pause.*)
> You like me to whisper to you. You like me to love you, whis-
> pering. Listen. You mustn't worry about . . . wives, husbands,
> things like that. It's silly. It's really silly. It's you, you now, here,
> here with me, here together, that's what it is, isn't it? You whis-
> per to me, you take tea with me, you do that, don't you, that's
> what we are, that's us, love me.

Vivien Merchant, with her warm whispers, was at her memorably
sexy best in this speech.

This is the first Pinter play in which there has been no violence.
All we get are conflicts of will, as in Richard's attempt to abolish
the game, to merge the two parts he plays into one and the afternoons into the evenings. At first Sarah hates it when he uses phrases
as Richard which he's only entitled to use as Max, when he pulls out
the bongo drums from the cupboard where they're hidden and when
he goes into the park-keeper game and crawls to her under the table.
But the ending is typically ambiguous. He seduces her into joining
in the game with him and so he succeeds in making the two roles
into one, but instead of throwing out the infidelity-in-the-afternoon
fantasy, this seems just to be letting it encroach into the evenings.
The ambiguity is a delicate and suitable one, and this play couldn't
have taken us any further anyway.

TEA PARTY

The main weakness of *Tea Party* is that it doesn't seem to be working towards making a statement. Pinter's plays usually do make a statement, even when it's one that couldn't be translated into any other words than the words Pinter himself has used, as in *The Birthday Party*, or when it's built precariously over a manhole of doubt, as in *The Collection*, or when it's highly ambiguous, as at the end of *The Lover*. But in *Tea Party*, for the first time, the mystifications seem to be there for their own sake. We're constantly titillated by the hints that something is going to be unravelled, the implicit promise of a resolution which never comes. In *The Collection*, we don't need to know any more than we are told about the relationship between Harry and Bill, because nothing relevant hinges on it, but in *Tea Party* we do need to know more than we're told about the relationships between Disson and Wendy, his secretary, Diana, his wife, and Willy, her brother, because that's what the play is about, or seems to be.

As in *A Slight Ache* – which it also resembles in the way it presents 'affluence' – the hints of symbolically failing sight are confusing. The optician repeatedly tells Disson that there's nothing wrong with his eyes, while he himself is increasingly bothered by them and so are we, through the tricks that are played on us with the television cameras. When he's playing ping-pong with Willy, we suddenly see two balls bouncing towards him, and us. When one of his young sons is holding the wood for him to saw, the saw seems to be going right through the boy's fingers. And again we're forced into identifying with his failing eyesight when the television screen goes black and the dialogue goes on.

> WENDY: I'm here, Mr Disson.
> DISSON: Where?
> WENDY: You're looking at me, Mr Disson.
> DISSON: You mean my eyes are open?

These are effective and frightening moments, but wilfully cryptic.

There's obviously some connection between Disson's troubles with his eyes and the fact that he's only attractive to Wendy when he lets her blindfold him with her chiffon.

> Don't you like my chiffon any more, to put round your eyes? My lovely chiffon?
> (*Pause.*
>> *He sits still.*)
> I always feel like kissing you when you've got that on round your eyes. Do you know that? Because you're all in the dark.
> (*Pause.*)
>> Put it on.
> (*She picks up the chiffon and folds it.*)
>> I'll put it on . . . for you. Very gently.
> (*She leans forward. He touches her.*)
>> No – you mustn't touch me, if you're not wearing your chiffon.

This was a very good moment for Vivien Merchant, using the same seductive voice she used in the 'whispering time' speech in *The Lover,* but the hint that the man is only attractive to the woman if he acquiesces in being blind is neither developed nor integrated into the texture of the play. Our understanding of what's going on is blurred still further by the suggestion that Disson's other senses may be failing too. One of the most confusing moments of all comes when we're told that Diana has gone home and we know that Wendy is in the next-door room with Willy. We hear laughter, as if they're flirting together, then when Disson kneels down to look through the keyhole, Diana walks through the door. Tricks like this have their effect, but it's both cheap and confusing.

If the play contains any statements at all, it seems to be making them about marriage, but making them in a highly personal way, without wanting to communicate them to us. Marriage is certainly the main motif. After the opening interview with Wendy, who says she left her last job because her chief never stopped touching her, Disson announces that he's getting married tomorrow morning and the next two scenes are focused on the decision that Willy shall replace the best man, who's ill. At the reception after the ceremony, Willy, whose relationship with his sister is highly ambiguous, proposes a toast in honour of the groom by talking almost entirely about the

Harold Pinter

bride. *Tea Party* is like *The Collection* in the alignment of the four main characters. This time they're not divided clearly into two couples, with one of each becoming a threat to the peace of the other but when Diana becomes Willy's secretary, we get a criss-crossing of dependencies and loyalties, and personal insecurity figures a great deal in the tensions and conflicts which develop. But whereas, in *The Collection,* each character was clearly in focus (except perhaps Stella) here Wendy, Diana and Willy are all mysteriously out of focus while the focus on Disson, who's put squarely in the centre of the picture, is deliberately blurred by the way we're made to identify with his blurred vision. And as usual, we're given no insight into his motivations, which seem highly erratic. It's when he has most reason to be suspicious of Willy that he acts most generously towards him making gestures which are going to involve him more and more deeply with the man. After Willy's speech at the reception, which is implicitly so insulting to Disson, he offers him a job in the firm and it is when he is angry with him for whispering with Diana that he offers him a partnership. His intention may be to bribe Willy and his motivation may be anxiety. This could be a good point if it became clearer, but it's only seen in the same confused perspective as everything else.

The ending is the most confused and confusing of all. It is reminiscent of *The Birthday Party*. The blindfolding of Disson harks back to the game of blindman's-buff and the culmination of the whole play is the reduction of Disson to helpless passivity. But in *The Birthday Party,* the demolition of Stanley had a kind of rightness about it: it was a continuation in external terms of a tendency that had started inside Stanley, so that the choice of him as a victim wasn't entirely arbitrary. Disson, however, would never choose himself as a victim or see himself as a failure. No doubt there would be levels in such a man on which he does do both, but the play doesn't concern itself with exploring or explaining them.

The scene of the tea party is quite effective, with Disson ill and blind, isolated in a chair while the other guests eat and talk and enjoy themselves at his expense. But there's a puzzling scene in which Willy gets Diana and Wendy to lie down on Wendy's desk. From the expression on their faces, he seems to be making love to

60

them, but the television cameras were cheating by cutting out the full picture of whatever was going on and giving us only a close-up of their faces.

Willy, Wendy and Diana are now a mysterious triangle, while all the other characters are in pairs: the two old ladies at the buffet-table, Disson's parents, the optician and his wife and Disson's twin sons. Only Disson himself is on his own, with his eyes bandaged. Willy's persecution of him culminates in putting a ping-pong ball into his hand, which clutches it. The enigmatic end comes when a shoe drops to the floor at the base of Wendy's desk. We still have no idea what's been happening on top of the desk. At this, Disson falls to the floor in his chair, and everybody has great difficulty in getting him up. They try and fail to get him out of the chair. The last word is Diana's:

Can you hear me?
(*Pause.*)
Robert, can you see me?
(*Pause.*)
It's me. It's me, darling.
(*Slight pause.*)
It's your wife.
(*Close up Disson's eyes. Open.*)

THE HOMECOMING

In Pinter's third full-length play, *The Homecoming*, the subject is once again home. But this time the danger is inside and the victim comes from outside. The occupants are more aggressive and destructive than ever before (an ex-butcher, a pimp, and a demolition worker who wants to go professional as a boxer) and the victim is an outsider who was at one time an insider, a member of the family who left home and now suffers by losing his wife when he brings her on a visit to the all-male ménage. The fear of losing a woman has been thematic in earlier plays, though less explicitly. The blind negro in *The Room* is a threat to Bert's ownership of Rose with his luring line 'Come home, Sal'. Stanley in *The Birthday Party* and Wally in *A Night Out* would probably have never made it with their girls anyway, but in so far as they lose them, it's to an older man. James in *The Collection* derives pleasure as well as pain from the idea of Stella's infidelity with Bill, and Richard in *The Lover* has to invent an infidelity on the part of his wife. In *Tea Party*, Disson's hold over both Diana and Wendy is threatened by Willy, though Willy's relationships with the two women are never clarified.

In *The Homecoming*, once again the play opens with a one-sided conversation. The speaker is the father who has taken over the role of mother. Max's nagging, repetitive way of talking and Lenny's hostile indifference are established right from the start.

> MAX: What have you done with the scissors?
> (*Pause.*)
> I said I'm looking for the scissors. What have you done with them?
> (*Pause.*)
> Did you hear me? I want to cut something out of the paper.
> LENNY: I'm reading the paper.
> MAX: Not that paper. I haven't even read that paper. I'm talking about last Sunday's paper. I was just having a look at it in the kitchen.
> (*Pause.*)

> Do you hear what I'm saying? I'm talking to you! Where's the
> scissors?
>
> LENNY (*looking up, quietly*): Why don't you shut up, you daft
> prat?

Max ignores the fact that he's being insulted and ignored and goes on
reminiscing, filling in a good deal more plot background of past
history than is usual in Pinter.

> I used to knock about with a man called MacGregor. I called him
> Mac. You remember Mac? Eh? Huhh! We were two of the worst
> hated men in the West End of London. I tell you, I still got the
> scars. We'd walk into a place, the whole room'd stand up, they'd
> make way to let us pass. You never heard such silence . . . He was
> very fond of your mother, Mac was. Very fond.

But the plotting is half-hearted and not very effective. The point of
it is to establish a parallel between the mother (who was unfaithful
to Max with MacGregor) and Ruth, who is quite willing to be set up
by the family as a whore. This may, for her, merely represent a
return to the kind of life she led before marrying a philosophy
teacher. If Teddy's mother was also a whore, as is suggested, Teddy's
choice of wife would be understandable, but underneath Pinter's
exaggeratedly casual treatment of the theme there is something
compulsive about the equations he keeps drawing between the
mother and the whore. As in *Tea Party*, he seems uncertain how far he
wants the meaning the play has for him to be clear to other people.

Max is in some ways reminiscent of Goldberg, talking sometimes
in the same rhythm but without the redeeming grain of humour in
the writing and without the fact of Jewishness ever being indicated
by anything but the names of the characters – Max, Lenny, Sam,
Joey, Teddy, Ruth.

Max is also reminiscent of Davies, particularly in the way he
talks about missed opportunities in his past. The new element in
characterization to the rapid self-contradiction in talking about his
dead wife and the self-deprecation.

> MAX: Mind you, she wasn't such a bad woman. Even though it
> made me sick just to look at her rotten stinking face, she wasn't
> such a bad bitch. I gave her the best bleeding years of my life,
> anyway.

FANNY: Plug it, will you, you stupid sod, I'm trying to read the paper.

MAX: Listen! I'll chop your spine off, you talk to me like that! You understand? Talking to your lousy filthy father like that!

Insults are thrown about like custard pies in the old comedies and Pinter writes them amusingly, never repeating himself.

The 63-year-old Uncle Sam also reminds us of Davies, with his self-important fantasies. He boasts of being the best chauffeur in the firm, the one that everybody asks for. The gentlest, weakest creature in this menagerie of a ménage, he's the butt of incessant raillery from Max, just as Max is from Lenny, but with the difference that Sam has been sexually frustrated all his life, which makes him vulnerable to jokes about weddings.

MAX: When you find the right girl, Sam, let your family know, don't forget, we'll give you a number one send-off, I promise you. You can bring her to live here, she can keep us all happy. We'd take it in turns to give her a walk round the park.

SAM: I wouldn't bring her here.

MAX: Sam, it's your decision. You're welcome to bring your bride here, to the place where you live, or on the other hand you can take a suite at the Dorchester. It's entirely up to you.

The dark hints of Max's sentence about giving her a walk round the park – the threat that Max and the family carry out against Teddy – again refer to the same recurrent motif, the fear of losing the woman.

With Lenny and Max we learn little about the surrounding circumstances of how they spend their lives; with Joey, the amateur boxer, and Sam, we learn perhaps too much – some of it is padding – but with Teddy and Ruth, when they arrive, we learn very little indeed. The dialogue is vague about what they are doing in England, where they've come from and how long they're staying. They're also erratic in their behaviour in a way quite different from that in which the family are erratic. Everything about the scene is improbable in a worrying way. Without having told anyone that they're coming, they arrive in the middle of the night and decide not to wake anyone up. At first Teddy tries to get Ruth to go to bed without him, saying that he wants to walk about for a few minutes. She then

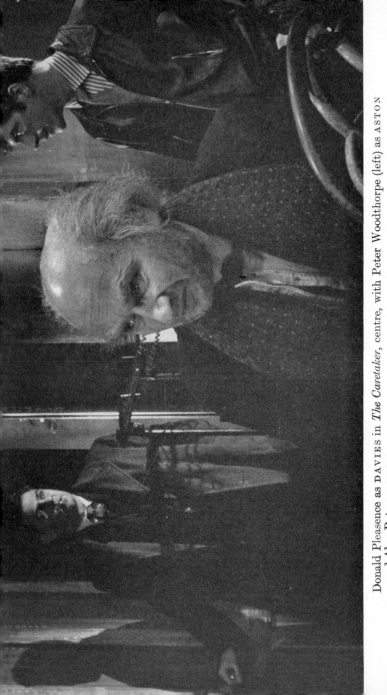

Donald Pleasence as DAVIES in *The Caretaker*, centre, with Peter Woodthorpe (left) as ASTON and Alan Bates as MICK.

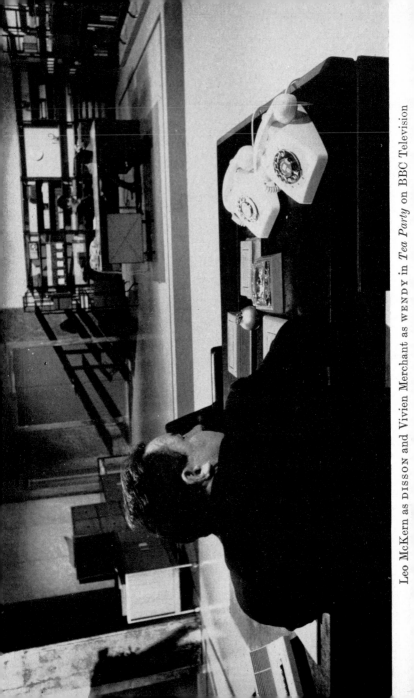

Leo McKern as DISSON and Vivien Merchant as WENDY in *Tea Party* on BBC Television decides that she wants to go for a walk and goes without him, leaving him alone for his scene with Lenny, who comes in wearing pyjamas, explaining that he sleeps down here now. 'Next door, I've got a kind of study, workroom-cum-bedroom next door now, you see.' Teddy says nothing about Ruth or being married and goes upstairs at the end of the scene, so that Ruth and Lenny can have a scene which starts off without either of them knowing who the other is. It leads into a mad monologue from Lenny which is like something out of *The Dwarfs*.

> LENNY: You must be connected with my brother in some way. The one who's been abroad.
> RUTH: I'm his wife.
> LENNY: Eh listen, I wonder if you can advise me. I've been having a bit of a rough time with this clock. The tick's been keeping me up. The trouble is that I'm not all that convinced it was the clock. I mean there are lots of things which tick in the night, don't you find that? All sorts of objects, which, in the day, you wouldn't call anything else but commonplace. They give you no trouble. But in the night any given one of a number of them is liable to start letting out a bit of a tick. Whereas you look at these objects in the day and they're just commonplace. They're as quiet as mice during the daytime. So . . . all things being equal . . . this question of me saying it was the clock that woke me up, well, that could very easily prove something of a false hypothesis.

Like so many things in the play, this speech is striking at the time but unexplained, arbitrary and structurally functionless. In the earlier Pinter, each part had its place in the architecture of a whole, but now, self-indulgent speeches like this are put in for the sake of deliberate mystification and immediate impact, irrespective of whether they contribute anything of value to the overall effect.

Lenny has a very long scene with Ruth and the conversation is unbalanced all through. Pinter is usually very good at unbalanced conversations, but this one doesn't work. After the clock speech,*

---

* Clocks often take on an unexpected importance in Pinter's plays. In *A Night Out* a clock is the weapon that Albert uses to threaten his mother and threaten the tart. In *The Caretaker,* one of Davies's main grudges against Aston is that he hasn't bought him a clock.

Harold Pinter

Lenny gives Ruth a glass of water which she hasn't asked for, inquires whether she minds his having one himself, interviews her about the holiday in Europe she's been having with Teddy and asks whether she minds if he holds her hand. When she says 'Why?', he answers 'I'll tell you why,' but goes off into a very long narrative speech about a night down by the docks when he met a woman who was falling apart with the pox and beat her up because she started taking liberties. Pinter doesn't allow Ruth to react to the surprising and irrelevant information except by taking on the role of interviewer: 'How did you know she was diseased?' For a while they switch roles and he interviews her: 'You and my brother are newly-weds, are you?' but we soon get back to a second long monologue from Lenny about an old woman who asked him to help her shift an iron mangle from one room to another. It was too heavy for him, so he told her to stuff it up her arse and gave her a short-arm jab to the belly. This is rather reminiscent of Walter's attempt in *Night School* to impress Sally by pretending to be a criminal, but this time we do not know whether to believe the story.

The trouble is that until the sexual game they start playing with the glass of water, when Ruth suddenly says 'If you take the glass, I'll take you' – and there's been nothing except the question about hand-holding to lead up to this – none of the conversation between Lenny and Ruth has anything to do with Lenny and Ruth. Not that Pinter's characters ever develop relationships with each other in the conventional way, but between Meg and Stanley, Davies and Aston, Bill and James, even Richard and Sarah, there is an interconnection in which the characters have a kind of consistency and a kind of freedom of choice. In *The Homecoming*, Pinter is making his characters behave quite arbitrarily, with an arbitrariness that is his, not theirs.

In the family there's nothing but the common predatoriness to link Lenny, Max and Joey together. Sam and Teddy are members of the family without having anything in common with it or with each other. Ruth is completely inscrutable both in relation to Teddy and to the family. Nobody's behaviour seems to be affected by anyone else's behaviour. In *Tea Party*, Disson's behaviour towards Willy was often the opposite of what would have been expected. In *The Homecoming*, the relationship between action and reaction is not even one of opposites. Almost nothing seems to happen as a reaction to anything else that happens. Everyone's behaviour consists of a series of unexpected, separate actions, each one either disconnected from the last or at a tangent with it, and the actions are separate, not only from each other, but from the personality of the protagonist. Harry in *The Collection* often behaved erratically but never lost his consistency. In *The Homecoming* it's only Teddy and Sam who have any consistency at all and in them it consists largely in the passivity with which they face the aggressions of their family. Lenny's only consistency is in his manner of speaking. Max hasn't even that amount of solidity, veering between animal mindlessness and a quite sophisticated badinage.

Quite apart from the implicit misanthropy, the undertone of the play is negative and pessimistic. In mood, it's rather like a *Troilus and Cressida* taken over entirely by Thersites and Pandarus.

> SAM: This is my house as well, you know. This was our mother's house.
> MAX: One lot after the other. One mess after the other.
> SAM: Our father's house.
> MAX: Look what I'm lumbered with. One cast-iron bunch of crap after another. One flow of stinking pus after another.
> (*Pause.*)
> Our father, I remember him. Don't worry. You kid yourself. He used to come over to me and look down at me. My old man did. He'd bend right over me, then he'd pick me up. I was only that big. Then he'd dandle me. Give me the bottle. Wipe me clean. Give me a smile. Pat me on the bum. Pass me around, pass me from hand to hand. Toss me up in the air. Catch me coming down. I remember my father.

And Max's bitterness against his father is echoed by Lenny's against him.

> I'll tell you what, Dad, since you're in the mood for a bit of a . . . chat, I'll ask you a question. It's a question I've been meaning to ask you for some time. That night . . . you know . . . the night you got me . . . that night with Mum, what was it like? Eh? When I was just a glint in your eye. What was it like? What was the background to it? I mean, I want to know the real facts about my background.

Harold Pinter

This unforgiving obsession with the moment of conception obviously stems from Beckett, whose characters adamantly refuse to forgive the 'accursed progenitor' for the irreversible act of bringing them into the world. Max's final reaction to Lenny is to spit at him, which is the right reaction, because the question is entirely impersonal. Max and Lenny aren't even related to each other by genuine hostility. The characters in this play are more isolated from each other than in any other play by Pinter, but he does nothing to put the isolation into perspective. Martin Esslin in his book *Pinter: A Study of His Plays* tries to interpret the play in terms of the Oedipal theme. After the expulsion of a father-figure by two sons in *The Caretaker*, the rivalry with a father-figure over a girl in *Night School* and after *The Lover*, in which 'the hero dreams of his wife (who is a mother) as a whore', Esslin says that it is in *The Homecoming* that the Oedipal theme emerges most fully and explicitly. 'It is as though it had gradually risen to the surface as Pinter gained the self-confidence and formal skill that enabled him to meet it head on rather than merely obliquely.' I would not have said that it was explicit in *The Homecoming* and it seems to me that where he treated it more obliquely, as in Stanley's relationship with Meg in *The Birthday Party* the results were better. Although we are told that Ruth is a mother - like Jessie she has three children – this does not make her theatrically effective as a mother-figure. She may be, as Esslin suggests, more like the dream mother of Lenny's and Joey's fantasies, still young and attractive, but the parallel between her and Jessie seems more verbally contrived than theatrically developed.

Even structurally, the climax of Act One is muffed. The scene in which Max bullies the pathetic Sam gets in the way of the long delayed confrontation between the married couple and the family. After so much rancour, so many squibs and thunderclaps of violence and threatened violence, we are so inured against the atmosphere of insults that it counts for very little when Max insults Ruth by calling her a tart. Whether he's right or not, whether she was one earlier or not is a question which in this perspective hasn't very much force. The actual violence, when it comes, comes, as we would by now expect, in an unexpected way. Max hits Joey in the stomach with all his strength and starts to collapse himself from the exertion of the blow. Sam goes to help him and for his pains gets hit on the head with Max's stick. The closing moment of the act is an equally enigmatic threat of tenderness between Max and Teddy as overloaded with menace as Ruth's threat of sex to Lenny.

> MAX: You want to kiss your old father? Want a cuddle with your old father?
> TEDDY: Come on, then.
> (*Teddy moves a step towards him.*)
>   Come on.
> (*Pause.*)
> MAX: You still love your old Dad, eh?
> (*They face each other.*)
> TEDDY: Come on, Dad. I'm ready for the cuddle.
> (*Max begins to chuckle, gurgling. He turns to the family and addresses them.*)
> MAX: He still loves his father!

Act Two starts with the phoney conviviality of the family reunion. Again a Jewish tone can be heard in Max's speeches as he rejoices, not without irony, in his three fine grown-up lads, wishing his dead wife could be there to see them. The tone changes rapidly into bitchiness and he plays the role of the wife nagging the husband to go out to work when he starts pitching into Sam, the unmasculine breadwinner. Then he gets back on his (and Pinter's) wedding hobby-horse, talking now to Teddy:

> MAX: Did you have a big function?
> TEDDY: No, there was no one there.
> MAX: You're mad. I'd have given you a white wedding. We'd have had the cream of the cream here. I'd have been only too glad to bear the expense, my word of honour.
> (*Pause.*)
> TEDDY: You were busy at the time. I didn't want to bother you.
> MAX: But you're my own flesh and blood. You're my first born. I'd have dropped everything.

One of the most effectively dramatic moments comes when Teddy, sensing that something is going to go wrong, tries to persuade Ruth to cut the visit short and go back with him to the States. But again

Harold Pinter

Teddy's manner of handling Ruth is very odd indeed, without coming into focus as indicative in any way of his relationship with her.

> TEDDY: . . . Look, I just brought you back to meet the family, didn't I? You've met them, we can go. The fall semester will be starting soon.
> RUTH: You find it dirty here?
> TEDDY: I didn't say I found it dirty here.
> (*Pause.*)
> I didn't say that.
> (*Pause.*)
> Look. I'll go and pack. You rest for a while. Will you? They won't be back for at least an hour. You can sleep. Rest. Please.
> (*She looks at him.*)
> You can help me with my lectures when we get back. I'd love that. I'd be so grateful for it, really. We can bathe till October. You know that. Here, there's nowhere to bathe, except the swimming bath down the road. You know what it's like? It's like a urinal. A filthy urinal!

Nobody realistically speaks to anybody else like that and the different kinds of departure from realism in this play haven't added up to any kind of convincing stylization.

After this, the play rapidly falls to pieces. There's an unpleasant scene in which Joey and Lenny simultaneously embrace Ruth while Teddy and Max both watch, without interfering. The scene blacks out after Teddy's speech about detachment, which I've quoted already. There's an odd scene about a cheese roll of Lenny's which Teddy has taken and eaten. It generates a kind of tension by its very oddness, but the tension is dissipated quickly when Lenny delivers a long homily to Teddy about it. It's amusing that Lenny should protest so strongly about losing his cheese roll when Teddy has been silent about losing his wife, but the irony isn't effective enough to sustain this speech for the length Lenny takes it to, although it's a good monologue as such. But what's missing is overall coherence. In *The Birthday Party*, we were made to care very much about what was happening to Stanley, without understanding it. Here we neither understand nor care.

70

Then the play becomes still more gratuitously unpleasant when Joey comes downstairs after being in bed with Ruth. He talks about it to Lenny and Teddy joins in the conversation. What follows as the family arrange to set Ruth up as a tart is rather like Giles Cooper's *Everything in the Garden* without the humour and without the feeling of inevitability. What happened there was highly improbable but one step led insidiously and convincingly to the next, and although Giles Cooper allowed himself considerable comic licence in representing the suburban types, they were incomparably more credible and more relevant to contemporary reality than Pinter's people. Even compared with his own early work, we miss the subtlety. In *The Birthday Party, The Room, The Dumb Waiter* and *The Caretaker,* there was always an inevitability in the development. Here it seems contrived.

The end is the worst of all. Sam announces that MacGregor had Max's wife in the back of his cab while he was driving it and then collapses on the floor. Teddy goes and Max has some kind of attack.

> (*He falls to his knees, whimpers, begins to moan and sob. He stops sobbing, crawls past Sam's body round her chair, to the other side of her.*)
> I'm not an old man.
> (*He looks up at her.*)
> Do you hear me?
> (*He raises his face to her.*)
> Kiss me.
> (*She continues to touch Joey's head, lightly. Lenny stands, watching.*)

THE BASEMENT

Originally conceived as a film, *The Basement* was made into a tele
vision play and transmitted in February 1967. It starts once again
with a contrast between the warmth and safety of a room, where
a man sits in an armchair reading a book, and the danger outside
where a man and a woman stand in the rain, hesitating before
ringing the doorbell, like animals about to pounce on their prey
Law, the man inside, shows himself to be an easy victim, lonely
glad to see Stott and hospitable to the extent of fussing.

> LAW: Here's a towel. Go on, give it a good wipe. That's it. You
> didn't walk here, did you? You're soaking. What happened to
> your car? You could have driven here. Why didn't you give me
> a ring? But how did you know my address? My God, it'
> years. If you'd have rung I would have picked you up. I would
> have picked you up in my car. What happened to your car?
> (*Stott finishes drying hair, puts towel on chair arm.*)
> STOTT: I got rid of it.
> LAW: But how are you? Are you well? You look well.
> STOTT: How are you?
> LAW: Oh, I'm well. Just a minute, I'll get you some slippers
> (*Goes to cupboard, bends.*) You're going to stay the night, aren'
> you? You'll have to, look at the time. I wondered if you'd eve
> turn up again. Really. For years. Here you are. Here's som
> slippers.
> (*Stott takes slippers, changes shoes.*)
> I'll find some pyjamas in a minute. Still, we'll have a cup o
> coffee first, or some . . . Or a drink? What about a drink
> You're not living at Chatsworth Road any more, are you?
> know that. I've passed by there, numbers of times. You'v
> moved. Where are you living now?
> STOTT: I'm looking for a place.

And he immediately invites him to stay for the night. But he doesn'
know about the girl outside. Oddly, Stott has left her standing in th
rain, which adds to the suspense and the mystery of how Law wil
be victimized, as he clearly will. The atmosphere of menace is un

mistakable. As soon as Stott brings the girl in, she starts undressing and gets into Law's bed. The host watches with some consternation, but all he can say is 'Can I get you some cocoa, some hot chocolate?' Stott gets into bed with her and starts to make love to her. Law picks up his book again.

The battle has begun. Stott – the name suggests stoat – uses his ownership of the woman to fight for possession of the room. Law fights to regain the ascendancy in a series of almost ritualized contests of strength. This is Pinter's version of 'The Games People Play', and Law – true to what his name suggests – plays the competitive games according to the rules, which puts him at a disadvantage. When they agree to have a race in a muddy field, Stott wins by not running. Looking back to see what has happened to him, Law falls and gets covered with mud. He is also half-hearted in his fight for possession of the woman. He wants her, and, as we see in the geographically unexplained seaside scenes, she responds to him. In fact she betrays Stott by trying to persuade Law to throw him out of the flat, but he turns down the chance of an alliance with her and betrays her betrayal to Stott, whom he still treats as a friend.

Both the aggression of the couple, who invade a man's house to make love in it, and the masochistic reaction of the victim are oddly close to what happens in Pinter's screenplay for the film *Accident,* based on Nicholas Mosley's novel. Coming back to his house after a visit to London, Stephen finds that Charlie and Anna have broken in to make love there. Stephen, who desires Anna, seems to be aware of the action as a kind of aggression and he is very angry, but we only hear the anger in the tone of voice he uses to stop Anna from making the bed. He tells her to leave it for the woman who comes in the mornings, but a moment later we see him making it himself. Then, going down the stairs with Charlie, he gives him a key of the house and invites him to use it for the week-end.

There is also a parallel between the games that are played in the film and the games in *The Basement.* In both, aggressions are brought into a new kind of focus. In the tennis in the film, there is a kind of balance between the geniality on the surface and the violence which only sometimes breaks through, as if by accident, but the extraordinary game that the dinner-jacketed guests play with the cushion is openly violent. It is like a vicious form of rugger in which people are aiming to hurt each other, and the dignity of the country house and the groomed glitter of the guests are invaluable as counterpoint. The scene makes a very valid point about the aggressive competitiveness inherent in this sort of sociality.

Although the purpose and the method of the two scripts often coincide, *The Basement* departs much further from naturalism than *Accident*. Pinter gives himself complete freedom to develop the conflict in any way that occurs to him, and in doing so, he exploits the medium to the full, using only a minimum of words in the dialogue but laying down in his stage directions detailed and well-judged instructions about the set, which virtually becomes a character in the play. After Law has been making love to Jane on the beach, he returns to the flat with her to find it unrecognizable. Stott is in possession of it and Scandinavian furniture has been installed. No one says anything about the change. Later, when the hostility of the two men is out in the open, they duel with broken milk bottles. Not only are they both stripped to the waist but the room too is suddenly bare. Pinter gives himself the same freedom in cutting between the room and the seashore without trying to indicate how much time elapses between one scene and the next, and summer changes casually into winter when only a second has gone by. But the method succeeds and the logic of the growing hostility working up through the games gives the action all the consistency it needs.

This freedom of movement in time and space represents a new departure for Pinter. In some ways, it is a development of the games played in *The Lover,* but here it's not just a matter of the characters playing a game. The whole play joins in the game, and one game creates the next. When Jane praises the room, Stott objects that it's too bright and starts turning off lights. When he makes love to Jane in the bed, Law's only reaction is to immerse himself in a Persian love manual, but in the first scene on the beach, which follows immediately, Law shows Jane that he knows more about Stott than she does.

> LAW: He has a connection with the French aristocracy. He was educated in France. Speaks French fluently, of course. Have you read his French translations?

JANE: No.

LAW: Ah. They're immaculate. Great distinction. Formidable
scholar, Stott. Do you know what he achieved at Oxford? He
achieved a First in Sanskrit at Oxford. A First in Sanskrit!

JANE: How wonderful.

LAW: You never knew?

JANE: Never.

LAW: I know for a fact he owns three châteaux. Three superb
châteaux. Have you ever ridden in his Alvis? His Facel Vega?
What an immaculate driver. Have you seen his yachts? Huh!
What yachts. What yachts.

The writing here reminds us of the 'true or false' game that Pinter
has played with us so often, and the half-teasing tone is a bit like
James's in *The Collection*, talking to Stella about Bill. Law is both
hinting at a friendship between Stott and himself, from which Jane
is excluded, and striking up a friendship with Jane, from which
Stott is excluded. The next development is that from making love
with Stott, Jane rolls over in the bed to smile at Law. Stott's next
move in taking over the room is to take down all the pictures while
Law looks on and agrees that they are terrible. This prepares the
ground for the surprise of the complete change of décor in the flat
which is to come later. There is a pleasantly casual piece of one-
upmanship from Stott in conversation with Law about Jane.

STOTT: She comes from a rather splendid family, actually.

LAW: Really?

STOTT: Rather splendid.

(*Pause.*)

LAW: Very helpful, of course, around the house.

STOTT: Plays the harp, you know.

LAW: Well?

STOTT: Remarkably well.

LAW: What a pity I don't possess one. You don't possess a
harp, do you?

STOTT: Oh, yes. I've got a harp.

LAW: A recent acquisition?

STOTT: No, I've had it for years.

And of course Stott goes on making love to Jane in the bed after Law
has started making love to her on the beach. In the restaurant scene,

Stott scores a point by changing to Campari after Law has told the waiter that they all want the same again. And this is followed by the race scene. There is a winter scene in the yard – a circle of footprints in the snow, as if one prisoner has been exercising – with Law trying weakly to persuade Stott that the flat is too small for three people, that the council would object, and so would the church. Stott stone-walls the approach, and we see no release of aggression from Law until the summer scene in which he starts throwing gramophone records at the wall, looking for some Debussy which Stott wants. When he finds it and turns round with it in his hand, it is winter again and the room has reverted to its original furnishing. After the whispering scene, when Law betrays Jane's betrayal to Stott, there is a scene rather reminiscent of Strindberg's *The Dance of Death,* with Stott apparently dying in bed and Jane and Law debating what to do with him. Then we see them in the corner 'snuffling each other like animals', as Pinter's direction puts it. We never learn whether he was ill, or pretending, or why, but the next game is played with a recorder. Law irritates Stott deliberately by walking about the room, first playing it, then singing through it. Stott throws a bowl of fruit across the room and then, picking up a marble, prepares to bowl to Law, who readily responds by pretending to bat with the recorder. Stott barks the word 'Play!' and as the sound crashes into the long silence, the marble crashes into the window. They go on playing, even after a marble hits Law in the face, drawing blood. Law wins the next point by batting a marble into the fishtank – water rushes out and we see a fish flapping about on the floor – but Stott knocks Law out with a final marble on the forehead. This is the last game before the duel with milk bottles, which reaches its climax in a close-up of the two jagged circles of glass crunching into each other. After this the starting positions are reversed. Stott is in possession of the room, which is furnished as at the beginning, and we see him in the arm-chair reading a book. Law is now in possession of Jane. We see them outside in the rain, preparing to ring. The closing words of the play are the same as the opening words, with the roles reversed and the characters reversed. Stott looks more like an easy victim; Law looks more dangerous.

It would have been impossible to contain all this within an hour of television without enormous economy and control. Visually it is richer and more varied than any of Pinter's other television plays and although many of the scenes could only have been shot by pre-filming, it exploits the possibilities of television to the full. While Pinter's dialogue, always spare, is pared down to a minimum, there is no mystification for the sake of keeping the audience guessing; what mystification there is serves the useful purpose of focusing our attention away from the surface of events and away from casual connections between them, on to the fears and anxieties and aggressions that are expressed in the actions and reactions, the playing and the fighting. We may start off by thinking 'how odd' when Jane undresses, but soon we are following each move in the manœuvring for superiority as if we were watching a wrestling match, and the tension is all the greater for the fact that there are no rules in the game – or if Law thinks there are, then Stott knows that there is no penalty for breaking them.

Altogether the piece is rather like a Debussy prelude: the structure may appear to be arbitrary but is satisfying because it has a logic of its own.

LANDSCAPE

After *The Homecoming*, which was written in 1964, Pinter did not believe he would ever produce another full-length play. 'My plays are getting shorter,' he said in an interview printed in *The Times*, 'words are so tender. One-act plays are all I seem to be able to write at the moment. I doubt if I will ever write something mammoth.' In this he seemed to resemble Beckett who has not written a full-length play since *Happy Days* (1961).

Landscape lasts only thirty minutes. There are two characters, but there is no dialogue between them. We alternate between their two monologues. Duff talks of Beth* as 'you' but most of the time he seems to be thinking of her rather than addressing her. She talks about her man and an experience with him on a beach when she was naked under her beachrobe and whispered to him about having his child. But we are never altogether certain whether this man was Duff or someone else.

Landscape was written for the stage, but because the Lord Chamberlain objected to the work 'fuck' and because Pinter refused to remove it, the play was premièred on the radio in April 1968. It was finally staged in July 1969, after the abolition of theatrical censorship †. But probably radio is the ideal medium for it, as it might have been for Beckett's *Play*, which is similar in keeping its characters immobile and having no physical action at all.

In *Play* all the action and in *Landscape* nearly all of it is set in the past. Pinter places his characters not in unlocalized urns but in the kitchen of a country house. His stage directions stipulate that 'the background of a sink, stove, etc., is dim' and though Guy Vaesen's production started with an announcer's voice telling us where we were and that Beth was in an armchair and Duff in a chair at the

* Vivien Merchant was playing Lady Macbeth at Stratford-on-Avon and Pinter was writing *Mac* but the joke about the missing 'Mac' in the two names has no apparent bearing on anything in the text and in any case neither name is ever mentioned.

† In a double bill with *Silence* at the Aldwych Theatre.

Landscape

table, the subsequent sound effects (introduced quite separately from
the dialogue in well-defined pauses) seemed to generalize us away
from the kitchen – gulls, a church bell, the lowing of cattle, a tractor,
a plane, sparrows, a car. But all the sounds very faint. And though
the house is important in their past – they were housekeeper and
handyman to a Mr Sykes but he's no longer there and recently
they've had it to themselves – the dialogue which makes up the
action (or the non-dialogue which makes up the non-action) could
equally well be spoken anywhere. The characters are much more
alive than Beckett's in *Play* – they have a present and a future as
well as a past, they have desires, impulses, moods – but the action
consists entirely of words and sounds.

The stage directions tell us that neither of them hears the other's
voice and that Beth never looks at Duff, but the ambiguity about
whether or not it is him she is talking about – like all the other
ambiguities of their relationship – is served well by radio. With
Peggy Ashcroft and Eric Porter in the parts, we were able to
feel that speech was a convention by which they were both com-
municating their silent thoughts directly to us, not speaking out loud
at all.

As in *Play*, the story is presented non-sequentially and impression-
istically as flotsam from the relationship that the characters have
shared washes up on the waves of present consciousness.

DUFF: I was thinking . . . when you were young . . . you didn't
laugh much. You were . . . grave.
(*Silence.*)
BETH: That's why he'd picked such a desolate place. So that I
could draw in peace. I had my sketch book with me. I took
it out. I took my drawing pencil out. But there was nothing
to draw. Only the beach, the sea.
(*Pause.*)
Could have drawn him. He didn't want it. He laughed.
(*Pause.*)
I laughed, with him.
(*Pause.*)
I waited for him to laugh, then I would smile, turn away, he
would touch my back, turn me, to him. My nose . . . creased.
I would laugh with him, a little.

(*Pause.*)

He laughed. I'm sure of it. So I didn't draw him.

DUFF: You were a first-rate house-keeper when you were young. Weren't you? I was very proud.

It also emphasizes the distance between them that they live in such different mental climates. She talks of snoozing in the sun, and sea and sand-dunes. He talks of walking the dog in the rain, puddles, pubs, mud, shit.

He remembers a time when he was unfaithful to her and told her about it afterwards. He also talks of being proud of her and how the boss trusted her. But primarily he talks of actions, things he has done and things that have happened to him in the past, things to be done in the future. She is less practical, more self-involved, more of a dreamer. Her only allusion to the future is to the time when she will no longer be beautiful, but she is already in her late forties and living in the past so much (in this empty house with no master to make her do the housework) she seems to think of herself as younger, more beautiful than she is. She is apparently childless and this episode on the beach, which could have led to childbirth, obsesses her. The deepest of the play's ironies is that the ambiguity about the man becomes fairly unimportant. Whether or not Duff was the man with her on the beach, the man in her memory is nothing to do with Duff as he is now. As with Stella in *The Collection*, it matters very little whether she has made love to another man or not. In either case the infidelity that Duff remembers pales to nothing by the side of the infidelity to him that is still going on. They have lived together for a long time but while he is – at least to some extent – still relating to her as she really is, either she has never related to him, or else stopped long ago. And there is a further irony in his enjoyment of the final abandonment of the attempt at communication.

At least now . . . at least now, I can walk down to the pub in peace and up to the pond in peace, with no one to nag the shit out of me.

Even though the play may not fully communicate all these ironies to the listener who only hears it once, it succeeds immediately in establishing the contrasts between the two mental landscapes, between the preoccupations of the two characters. Both Beth and Duff use words very effectively to create their own personalities, defining themselves both by the words they choose and by the pictures they paint with them:

> DUFF: Do you remember the weather yesterday? That downfall?
> BETH: He felt my shadow. He looked up at me standing above him.
> DUFF: I should have had some bread with me. I could have fed the birds.
> BETH: Sand on his arms.
> DUFF: They were hopping about. Making a racket.
> BETH: I lay down by him, not touching.
> DUFF: There wasn't anyone else in the shelter. There was a man and woman, under the trees, on the other side of the pond. I didn't feel like getting wet. I stayed where I was.
> (*Pause.*)
> Yes, I've forgotten something. The dog was with me.
> (*Pause.*)
> BETH: Did those women know me? I didn't remember their faces. I'd never seen their faces before. I'd never seen those women before. I'm certain of it. Why were they looking at me? There's nothing strange about me. There's nothing strange about the way I look. I look like anyone.

This total dependence on words is new for Pinter. Even in the three earlier plays which were written for radio (*A Slight Ache*, *A Night Out* and *Night School*) he relied more on action and less on the way the words hit the listener's ear. What is certain is that he could never have written *Landscape* had he not had so much experience of thinking in radio terms.

SILENCE

Silence was not planned as a sequel to *Landscape*. 'It was one of those happy things that rarely happen with me,' Pinter said in an interview quoted in *The Times*, 'I always feel after completing something that I'll never write again, but then came *Silence*. It took a long time to write – longer in fact than any full-length play of mine.'

Landscape and *Silence* together run less than two hours but this pleases Pinter. 'I think evenings in the theatre tend to go on too long. I feel the audience will have quite enough with mine. They'll be glad to get out; they won't want any more. . .'

Landscape and *Silence* branch out quite a long way from the main trunk of Pinter's work. They make him seem rather like a symphonic composer turning to chamber music – Boulez-like music in which the intervals between the notes are almost more important than the notes themselves. Like Beckett in his later plays, Pinter is trying to draw not more but less on the resources which the medium offers. *Landscape* has no movement at all, *Silence* has only very little, and the characters are less often talking to each other than talking to themselves about themselves. They have had and are still having relationships, but there is no direct attempt to dramatize the relationships. So there is no action, only the sketchiest suggestion of plot, no violence and none of the atmosphere of menace which was characteristic of all the plays from *The Room* to *The Homecoming*.

Altogether the physical world becomes less important than the mental world in which the characters live. The room is no longer a haven of apparent safety from the dangers of the world outside or an arena for a battle about territorial rights. Each of the three characters in *Silence* has an area with a bed, a table and a chair in it. The stage direction makes no mention of walls and if there are walls they will not be important as frontiers. The locale defined by the designer no longer matters: the scenery is created by the words. What Pinter is giving us now is a three-dimensional poetry, a dialogue in which the words do more of the work than ever before in his plays.

In *Silence* there are two men and a girl. Ellen is in her twenties, Rumsey is forty, and Bates in his mid-thirties. Rumsey's opening monologue, with its references to colours, weather and movements, immediately creates a vivid impression of his mental world.

> I walk with my girl who wears a grey blouse when she walks and grey shoes and walks with me readily wearing her clothes considered for me. Her grey clothes.
> She holds my arm.
> On good evenings we walk through the hills to the top of the hill past the dogs the clouds racing just before dark or as dark is falling when the moon
> When it's chilly I stop her and slip her raincoat over her shoulders or rainy slip arms into the arms, she twisting her arms. And talk to her and tell her everything.
> She dresses for my eyes.
> I tell her my thoughts. Now I am ready to walk, her arm in me her hand in me.
> I tell her my life's thoughts, clouds racing. She looks up at me or listens looking down. She stops in midsentence, my sentence, to look up at me. Sometimes her hand has slipped from mine, her arm loosened, she walks slightly apart, dog barks.

Ellen's monologue, which follows, also refers to weather, to walking and to dogs. She is talking of the men in her life.

> There are two. One who is with me sometimes, and another. He listens to me. I tell him what I know. We walk by the dogs. Sometimes the wind is so high he does not hear me. I lead him to a tree, clasp closely to him and whisper to him, wind going, dogs stop, and he hears me.
> But the other hears me.

Bates, the other man in her life, speaks in a rhythm which contrasts with Rumsey's rhythm rather as Duff's contrasts with Beth's in *Landscape*. The cadences are shorter, the manner rougher, brusquer. The emphasis is on taking her, holding her, whereas Rumsey was content to walk apart. And whereas Rumsey spoke of natural scenery, Bates talks of the town. The dog image here extends to the cars.

> Caught a bus to the town. Crowds. Lights round the market,

Harold Pinter

rain and stinking. Showed her the bumping lights. Took her down around the dumps. Black roads and girders. She clutching me. This way the way I bring you. Pubs throw the doors smack into the night. Cars barking and the lights. She with me, clutching.

Brought her into this place, my cousin runs it. Undressed her, placed my hand.

Rumsey seems less anxious to dominate Ellen, more patient, gentler and more willing to empathize with her.

She walks from the door to the window to see the way she has come, to confirm that the house which grew nearer is the same one she stands in, that the path and the bushes are the same, that the gate is the same. When I stand beside her and smile at her, she looks at me and smiles.

BATES: How many times standing clenched in the pissing dark waiting? The mud, the cows, the river.
You cross the field out of darkness. You arrive.
You stand breathing before me. You smile.
I put my hands on your shoulders and press. Press the smile off your face.

Rumsey enjoys reading and watching the clouds. He likes silence Bates resents noise but lives surrounded by it.

I'm at my last gasp with this unendurable racket. I kicked open the door and stood before them. Someone called me Grandad and told me to button it. It's they should button it. Were I young . . .
One of them told me I was lucky to be alive, that I would have to bear it in order to pay for being alive, in order to give thanks for being alive.
It's a question of sleep. I need something of it, or how can I remain alive, without any true rest, having no solace, no constant solace, not even any damn inconstant solace.
I am strong, but not as strong as the bastards in the other room, and their tittering bitches, and their music, and their love.
If I changed my life, perhaps, and lived deliberately at night, and slept in the day. But what exactly would I do? What can be meant by living in the dark?

For all three characters, the emphasis is on solitude. Ellen speaks about an elderly woman who tries to be friendly and quizzes her about her sexual experiences. But Ellen holds back from her.

> I'm old, I tell her, my youth was somewhere else, anyway I don't remember. She does the talking anyway.

After all these monologues, Bates moves to Ellen and in a repetitious dialogue of very short lines tries, unsuccessfully, to persuade her to come out.

BATES: Come with me tonight.
ELLEN: Where?
BATES: Anywhere. For a walk.
(*Pause.*)
ELLEN: I don't want to walk.
BATES: Why not?
(*Pause.*)
ELLEN: I want to go somewhere else.
(*Pause.*)
BATES: Where?
ELLEN: I don't know.
(*Pause.*)
BATES: What's wrong with a walk?
ELLEN: I don't want to walk.

He goes on, puzzlingly, to talk to her about his cousin's place as if he had never mentioned it to her before. This throws doubt on his first monologue in which he said he took her there. Perhaps he was talking about another girl. Perhaps he was talking about Ellen but only imagined he took her. Perhaps he actually took her but is nevertheless talking as if he didn't expect her to remember the place. Perhaps the sequence in which we are watching events is not the sequence in which they happened. Just as the ambiguity focuses our attention on what is going on under the surface of events, so, with speech, Pinter is not mimicking or tape-recording but listening for the movements that go on under the surface.

BATES: I walk in my mind. But can't get out of the walls, into a wind. Meadows are walled, and lakes. The sky's a wall. Once I had a little girl. I took it for walks. I held it by its hand. It looked up at me and said, I see something in a tree,

Harold Pinter

> a shape, a shadow. It is leaning down. It is looking at us.
> Maybe it's a bird, I said, a big bird, resting. Birds grow tired,
> after they've flown over the country, up and down in the wind,
> looking down on all the sights, so sometimes, when they reach
> a tree, with good solid branches, they rest.

Poetry is used, like this, to draw in the contours on the play's
map of the character's mental scenery. But this is not its only use.
There is a short passage between Rumsey and Ellen in which the
language, partly by its rhythm, partly by its meaning, suggests
love-making.

> ELLEN: When I run . . . when I run . . . when I run . . . over the
> grass . . .
> RUMSEY: She floats . . . under me. Floating . . . under me.
> ELLEN: I turn. I turn. I wheel. I glide. I wheel. In stunning
> light. The horizon moves from the sun. I am crushed by the
> light.

But this suggestion of contact is immediately followed by a passage
about non-contact, as if the whole of life were lived on a parabola
of non-meeting.

> Sometimes I see people. They walk towards me, no, not so,
> walk in my direction, but never reaching me, turning left, or
> disappearing, and then reappearing, to disappear into the wood.
> So many ways to lose sight of them, then to recapture sight of
> them. They are sharp at first sight . . . then smudged . . . then
> lost . . . then glimpsed again . . . then gone.

And further doubts about the nature of the contact that exists
between Rumsey and Ellen is raised by the dialogue which follows,
when she moves to his area. She notices that he has painted it and
made shelves. The dialogue then makes the point that she has not
been there since she was a little girl. There is also the suggestion of a
little girl talking to a grown man in the way they speak to each other.
As in her dialogue with Bates, the lines are kept very short.

> RUMSEY: Look at your reflection.
> ELLEN: Where?
> RUMSEY: In the window.
> ELLEN: It's very dark outside.
> RUMSEY: It's high up.

ELLEN: Does it get darker the higher you get?
RUMSEY: No.

As the play goes on, age seems to become more fluid and more metaphorical. Bates tells us of his landlady's asking him whether he is 'nothing but a childish old man'. Ellen asks herself whether she is old. Far removed though the play is from *The Room*, the characters' uncertainty about age seems to belong to the same order as Mr Kidd's uncertainty about how many floors there are in the house. Essentially there is no way of measuring. You can only measure if you can relate and none of them can. They are all alone among other people, surrounded by silence which their speech does nothing to break. Ellen asks herself whether she is silent or speaking. When she goes to Rumsey and he advises her to find a young man, she first says that there aren't any, then that she doesn't like them. That she has been married is mentioned only to show how unimportant it is.

> My drinking companion for the hundredth time asked me if I'd ever been married. This time I told her I had. Yes, I told her I had. Certainly. I can remember the wedding.

Bates's little girl is similarly unimportant.

As the play approaches its end, the sections of monologue become shorter, there are more reprises of fragments from earlier dialogue and the juxtapositions become more pointed. *Silence* is neither like one poem spoken by three voices nor like three poems devised to intersect. It is like a totally new kind of dramatic poem in which the relationships between the three kinds of poetry are clearer and more important than the relationships between the three characters on the level of action and physical contact.

NIGHT

Night is a sketch which runs for seven minutes and only took forty minutes to write. 'I was sitting with my wife after lunch. Normally I fall asleep, but on this occasion I suddenly got up, went upstairs and wrote *Night*. It came so easily.'

It is less complex than *Silence* and closer in theme and form to *Landscape*, but comic. There is no movement but it kept the audience at the Comedy Theatre in incessant fits of laughter.

A man and a woman in their forties are sitting at a table with their coffee. They are speaking to each other about memories of shared experience which come nowhere near to coinciding.

> MAN: We stopped and looked down at the river. It was night. There were lamps lit on the towpath. We were alone. We looked up the river. I put my hand on the small of your waist. Don't you remember? I put my hand under your coat.
> (*Pause.*)
> WOMAN: Was it winter?
> MAN: Of course it was winter. It was when we met. It was our first walk. You must remember that.
> WOMAN: I remember walking. I remember walking with you.
> MAN: The first time? Our first walk?
> WOMAN: Yes, of course I remember that.
> (*Pause.*)
> WOMAN: We walked down a road into a field, through some railings. We walked to a corner of the field and then we stood by the railings.
> MAN: No. It was on the bridge that we stopped.
> (*Pause.*)
> WOMAN: That was someone else.

As in *Landscape* and *Silence*, Pinter is no longer imitating colloquial speech. 'There was no sound,' the man says when the woman thinks she hears a child crying. 'The house is silent.' And as in *Landscape*, the barest outline of present circumstances is elaborately filled in with talk about the past. But through this talk, the essentials about the present relationship are created, very funnily, especially in the discussion about how he touched her.

> MAN: I touched your breasts.
> WOMAN: Where?
> MAN: On the bridge. I felt your breasts.
> WOMAN: Really?
> MAN: Standing behind you.
> WOMAN: I wondered whether you would, whether you wanted to, whether you would.
> MAN: Yes.
> WOMAN: I wondered how you would go about it, whether you wanted to, sufficiently.
> MAN: I put my hands under your sweater, I undid your brassiere, I felt your breasts.
> WOMAN: Another night perhaps. Another girl.
> MAN: You don't remember my fingers on your skin?
> WOMAN: Were they in your hands? My breasts? Fully in your hands?
> MAN: You don't remember my hands on your skin?
> (*Pause.*)
> WOMAN: Standing behind me?
> MAN: Yes.
> WOMAN: But my back was against railings. I felt the railings .. behind me. You were facing me. I was looking into your eyes. My coat was closed. It was cold.
> MAN: I undid your coat.
> WOMAN: It was very late. Chilly.

They are disagreeing less now, but significantly, it is just after he has mentioned that they walked down the tow-path to a rubbish-dump that she says he had her. He promised to adore her always and he says that he does. They had children, which are mentioned as casually as the child in *Silence*. The final emphasis is on her suspicion that his memories of her merge into his memories of other women and his suspicion that her memories of him merge into memories of other men. This comes in a passage in which they talk about their present conversation as if it were one of many in the past.

> WOMAN: And we sat and talked and you remembered women on bridges and towpaths and rubbish dumps.

Harold Pinter

MAN: And you remembered your bottom against railings and men holding your hands and men looking into your eyes.

WOMAN: And talking to me softly.

MAN: And your soft voice. Talking to them softly at night.

WOMAN: And they said I will adore you always.

MAN: Saying I will adore you always.

Both of them seem quite content to digest their jealousy. Complacent about it, almost.

OLD TIMES

In an interview for the radio recorded in September 1970, while he was still working on *Old Times*, Pinter described how he started it. 'I was lying down on a sofa. I was reading a paper. And I did suddenly sit up, dashed upstairs. No reason at all. Nothing to do with what I was reading . . . And started to write. Two characters appeared on paper. I knew nothing about them. I've learned. I'm learning quite a bit about them . . . When I write I don't consider whether the characters are able to communicate or not able or in what way they're doing so or not doing so . . . I try to simply proceed from moment to moment between the characters and indeed the silences that fall between them . . . My job, as I see it, is really to shape an image on the stage. Let it live, but shape it in dramatic terms and leave it at that. I have nothing else to say. I'm only interested in the characters in that given situation.'

It follows that the questions 'What does it mean?' and 'What is the play about?' are equally liable to be dangerous, inviting a misleading translation of the images and the relationships into conceptual terms. A play like *Old Times* may give rise to a great many questions, philosophical and ontological questions, questions about time, memory and reality, but it is neither the play's purpose nor duty to suggest answers. The questions, rather, are part of a tremendously sophisticated game with the audience. For there are always two given situations: one between the characters, the other between the play and the audience. Pinter, of course, is by now very well aware of the attempts that will be made to impose meanings on each play he writes. He tries to remain immune to the pressure of audience expectations, and while he was writing *Old Times* he did not know whether it had any relation to any of his previous work. But there is no such thing as a non-relationship with the audience you are writing for; in holding back from it – perhaps even to help himself to hold back from it – Pinter gently teases it. The characters also tease each other, and the two kinds of teasing overlap.

As the lights go up on Deeley and Kate in their converted farmhouse,

Harold Pinter

a third figure, Anna, is in the background, dimly lit, looking out of the window. The other two, who are waiting for her, talk about her as if she is not there. But later, when she begins talking to Kate about the time, twenty years ago, when they were sharing an apartment and working as secretaries, it is clear that her move downstage (to join the others in the brighter light) is not meant to represent an entrance. She has heard them talking about the casserole that Kate has cooked.

> ANNA: You have a wonderful casserole.
> DEELEY: What?
> ANNA: I mean wife. So sorry. A wonderful wife.
> DEELEY: Ah.
> ANNA: I was referring to the casserole. I was referring to your wife's cooking.

Anna uses words like 'lest' and 'gaze', which, according to Deeley, are no longer used very often. Later, after he has described his first meeting with Kate in a cinema at a showing of *Odd Man Out*, she says:

> There are some things one remembers even though they may never have happened. There are things I remember which may never have happened but as I recall them so they take place.

She goes on to describe how she once found Kate in the bedroom with a man who was sobbing, and later saw him on her bed, lying across her lap. She also talks about Sicily, where she says she is living, and about her husband. Abruptly, after a silence, she and Kate are discussing whether they should stay in or go out for the evening, talking to each other as if we had been transported back to the time when they were living together. But it is not a flashback because Deeley is able to interrupt, and his line 'Hungry? After that casserole?' implies, on the contrary, a flash-forward to the time after dinner. As the act ends, he is the odd man out, for Anna, who is persuading Kate to stay in, is offering to invite a man over and suggesting various names, none of which are his. Kate will have a bath and decide, while doing so, which man should be asked over. Anna offers to run the bath for her, but no, tonight she will run it for herself.

As the lights go up on Act Two we are still in the farmhouse but upstairs in the bedroom. Kate is in the bathroom, and Anna is sitting on one of the two divans. Deeley comes in with coffee and though the beginning of Act One implied that he had never met her, his first speech in Act Two ends 'You prefer it white with sugar, I believe?' The suggestion that he has, in fact, met her before is developed almost immediately, when he tells her he remembers her from a pub just off the Brompton Road and a party at someone's flat in Westbourne Grove.

> DEELEY: You sat on a very low sofa, I sat opposite and looked up your skirt. Your black stockings were very black because your thighs were so white. . . . I simply sat sipping my light ale and gazed . . . gazed up your skirt. You didn't object, you found my gaze perfectly acceptable.

He also says he remembers seeing a girl-friend of hers, who sat on the sofa with her at the party. After Kate reappears, fresh from her bath, Deeley refers again to *Odd Man Out*, comparing the smile on her face now with her smile when they walked down the street together after the film. Then Kate and Anna are again talking to each other as if they were still bachelor girls in London, discussing men and which one to invite round for the evening. And again Deeley interrupts, saying that one of them is out of town. After a silence, the conversation seems to switch back to the present place and the present time. In the play's opening conversation Kate had said that Anna used to steal bits and pieces from her, including underwear. Now Anna says that once she borrowed some of Kate's underwear to go to a party and was punished for her sin when a man spent the whole evening looking up her skirt.

> ANNA: But from that night she insisted, from time to time, that I borrow her underwear – she had more of it than I, and a far greater range – and each time she proposed this she would blush, but propose it she did, nevertheless. And when there was anything to tell her, when I got back, anything of interest to tell her, I told her.

Deeley becomes very angry about the claim Anna is making to such an intimate share in his wife's past. 'Sounds a perfect marriage,'

Harold Pinter

he sneers. Kate says very little, but sides with Anna, telling her husband that if he doesn't like it he can go. Deeley's reprisal is to tell her about his earlier acquaintance with Anna, ironically using mock-hippy language.

> DEELEY: We had a scene together. She freaked out. She didn't have any bread, so I bought her a drink. She looked at me with big eyes, shy, all that bit. She was pretending to be you at the time. Did it pretty well. Wearing your underwear she was too, at the time. . . . She thought she was you, said little, so little. Maybe she was you. Maybe it was you, having coffee with me, saying little, so little.

Kate now, suddenly, talks as if she knew everything about Deeley's relationship with Anna, who found his face, she says, sensitive, vulnerable, and wanted to comfort it in the way only a woman can. Anna, who had at first denied having any memory of Deeley, now coolly admits to remembering him well, and Kate, in what seems like a final fusillade of quiet aggression, tells Anna that she remembers her dead.

> KATE: You didn't know I was watching you. I leaned over you. Your face was dirty. You lay dead, your face scrawled with dirt, all kinds of earnest inscriptions, but unblotted, so that they had run, all over your face, down to your throat. . . . When you woke my eyes were above you, staring down at you. You tried to do my little trick, one of my tricks you had borrowed, my little slow smile, my little slow shy smile, my bend of the head, my half closing of the eyes, that we knew so well, but it didn't work. The grin only split the dirt at the sides of your mouth and stuck. . . . When I brought him into the room your body of course had gone. . . . He liked your bed and thought he was different in it because he was a man. But one night I said let me do something, a little thing, a little trick. . . . He thought I was going to be sexually forthcoming, that I was about to take a long promised initiative. I dug about in the windowbox, where you had planted our pretty pansies, scooped, filled the bowl, and plastered his face with dirt. He resisted . . . with force. He would not let me dirty his face, or smudge it, he wouldn't let me. He suggested a wedding instead and a change of environ-

ment. (*Slight pause.*) Neither mattered. (*Pause.*) He asked
me once, at about that time, who had slept in that bed before
him. I told him no one. No one at all.

This is the last word spoken, but after a long silence Anna walks to
the door and stops there, her back towards them. Deeley begins to
sob quietly. Anna switches off the lamps and lies down on one of
the divans. Kate is on the other. Deeley stands, looks at both divans,
goes to Anna's, goes to Kate's, sits, and then lies across her lap. He
gets up, slumps into the armchair. The lights come sharply up to a
maximum of brightness. As they dim the play is over.

But of course it is not over. The excited buzz of speculation which
starts in the auditorium after the first public preview and goes on
afterwards in conversations, in the newspapers, the weeklies, the
monthlies, the books – all this is in no sense separate from the play.
However hard Pinter tries to hold back from involvement with his
audience, the writing, the production, and the acting cannot have
developed without some consciousness of how people will react,
some calculation about how much to emphasize the various suggestions that the lines, the silences, and the movements make about
the relationships between the three characters.

Or are there only two? One interpretation is that Kate and Anna
are two different sides of the same woman, Anna representing
whatever survives of that part of the girlish self which seems to be
put aside on marrying. Another is that Anna is really dead but
lives on in the memories of the other two. For Harold Hobson of *The
Sunday Times*, who pronounced *Old Times* one of the finest plays of
its generation, Anna, who never leaves the stage, 'nevertheless is
never actually on the stage at all.' As Irving Wardle of *The Times*
saw the play, 'what it communicates intensely is the experience of
three people whose lives have arrested long before, and who are
searching for confirmation of the vital experiences that have faded
to trivial details and emptiness in their own memories.' For Ronald
Bryden, then of the *Observer*, 'the battleground is Kate: which of the
two, Deeley or Anna, has possessed more of her? The weapons, as
usual, are language and sex ... Truth has nothing to do with it.'
And he goes on to speculate about whether Anna really remembers a

man in the bedroom with Kate. 'As in *The Homecoming*,' he concludes, 'the final, devastating victory belongs to neither battler but to the woman battled over.'

All attempts to explain the play involve an attempt to summarize something unsummarizable, and most of them enter too ingenuously into the game of finding different degrees of truthfulness in different speeches. 'Yes I believed him when he said that, but she wasn't telling the truth when she said that.' No one in a play is telling the truth. None of the events happened in reality. But though we all know this very well, we still look for factual consistency in the fictional artifice that every play is, and Pinter is the first playwright fully to explore the theatrical potential of frustrating us.

The question of whether Anna really saw a man lying across Kate's lap is a meaningless question. What matters is the relationship between the words in which she speaks about it and the image we see at the end of the play when Deeley lies across Kate's lap. The question of whether Anna is alive or dead, an aspect of Kate, a separate person, or a set of memories in the minds of the other two is a question which deserves only a minimum of attention. It may not be wholly avoidable, but it does not need to be in the foreground of our minds; the criticism which sets out to bring it into the foreground is bad criticism. We go to the theatre with our responses preconditioned by what we have heard and what we have read. *Old Times* is not a puzzle to be solved; it is an elaborate construction of words, echoing silences and images which ought to be enjoyed as such. If it makes a statement – as every play, in some sense, must – it is a statement which could not have been made by Pinter in any other way, and which remains unparaphrasable. Murder plays are usually badly written and our interest in them exhausted as soon as the mystery is solved. *Old Times* is extremely well written, and the critic can best help us to relish the writing by weaning us away from trying to solve the mysteries.

MONOLOGUE

Monologue was written for television, but to make a man talk to an empty chair as if his friend were sitting in it is a device which is intrinsically more theatrical than televisual, and the play works better on the stage. The other medium in which it could succeed is radio, though it would come over as more realistic, for there would be no means of establishing the emptiness of the second chair. In any case, the words need to register with more force than they had in Christopher Morahan's television production (April 1973) which kept cutting between two cameras trained on the same face from different angles, sometimes letting the old image of it linger on the screen after the new one had appeared, and the rhythm of the inter-cutting did not reinforce the movement of the text. But when the same actor, Henry Woolf, played the part on the stage at two fringe theatres, the Orange Tree, Richmond, and the King's Head, Islington, the play seemed simpler and better.

Like Beckett's *Not I*, which was staged in New York in November 1972 and at the Royal Court in January 1973, *Monologue* presents one character's view of a series of events which are over before the play starts and which can exist only fragmentarily in the present tense. In *Not I* the fragmentation affects both the syntax and the monologuist's delivery of the words; Pinter's monologuist usually speaks in complete sentences, while his prose is less urgent and emotionally flatter than Beckett's.

Monologue seems to derive from *The Basement*. The story is based on a very similar triangular relationship, but with the colour of the girl's skin changed to black and with only one of the two men physically present. He talks to his absent rival about their friendship and about their girl. Again, competitive game-playing is used as an image of loving rivalry, but this time the games cannot be acted out. Rhetorical challenges are issued to the empty chair, and we get reminiscences about ping-pong, fives, putting and practice in the nets. As in the earlier television play, the games seem to have provided a safety-valve for the spirit of sibling competitiveness, and

97

Harold Pinter

there is the same ironical name-dropping that makes culture-heroes into counters:

> You introduced me to Webster and Tourneur, admitted, but who got you going on Tristan Tzara, Breton, Giacommetti and all that lot?

Stylistically *Monologue* is more in line with *Landscape* and *Silence*. Pinter is again renouncing all direct theatrical confrontation, and merging the exterior realities into the mental images. The action must be expressed through words, silences, rhythms, but he has neither fulfilled the promise of *Landscape* and *Silence* nor succeeded (as Beckett has in *Not I*) in creating a flow of words that generates sufficient emotional force to make the visual reductionism into an advantage. The rhythms of *Monologue* are less definite and less interesting than those of *Landscape* and *Silence*, while the phrasing is more colloquial. The clichés, even when they are inverted ironically (like 'the crap is cut') are too tired to produce the incisive impacts that are needed. Though we see nothing of Beckett's woman except her mouth, she manages to put herself into a very clear perspective; the self-irony of Pinter's man is not enough to save the play from emotional imprecision and even sentimentality.

The affectionate jealousy he feels towards his absent friend does become quite piquant when he tells him he ought to have been black.

> I often had the impression . . . often . . . that you two were brother and sister, some kind of link-up, some kind of identical shimmer, deep down in your characters, an inkling, no more, that at one time you had shared the same pot.

We gather that the speaker temporarily gained exclusive possession of the girl after his better-looking rival moved away from where they were living.

> I brought her to see you, after you'd pissed off to live in Notting Hill Gate. Naturally. They all end up there. I'll never end up there, I'll never end up on that side of the Park. (*Pause.*) Sitting there with your record player, growing bald, Beethoven, cocoa, cats. That really dates it. The cocoa dates it.

Monologue

Some of the phrases and repetitions are extremely forceful, but the three sentences before the pause are slack, and the selection of fragments, unlike Beckett's, often seems arbitrary. They arouse our curiosity without satisfying it, and the love between the two men, which is the underlying subject, is not sufficiently brought to the surface by the ending.

> You should have had a black face, that was your mistake. You could have made a going concern out of it, you could have chalked it up in the book, you could have had two black kids. (*Pause.*) I'd have died for them. (*Pause.*) I'd have been their uncle. (*Pause.*) I am their uncle. (*Pause.*) I'm your children's uncle. (*Pause.*) I'll take them out, tell them jokes. (*Pause.*) I love your children.

As in *The Basement*, the effectiveness of the ending depends on a reversal of roles. Having pictured the other man as the coloured girl's brother, the speaker is now picturing himself as the uncle of her children. Neat though it is, the point is not good enough to compensate for all that is failing to emerge.

THE SCREENPLAYS

In eighteen years of writing Pinter has produced only three or four full-length plays – whether *Old Times* is really a full-length play is questionable. But besides writing screenplays based on three of his plays *The Caretaker*, *The Birthday Party* and *The Homecoming*, he has written five screenplays based on fiction by other writers – *The Servant*, from a long short story by Robin Maugham; *The Pumpkin Eater*, from the novel by Penelope Mortimer; *The Quiller Memorandum* from the thriller called *The Berlin Memorandum* by Adam Hall; *Accident* from Nicholas Mosley's novel and *The Go-Between* from L. P. Hartley's.

His screenplays therefore bulk large in his work. Like most successful playwrights, he has probably earned very much more money from the cinema than he has from the theatre, and as a writer he has developed in the way that he has partly because of the work he has done in adapting other people's books for the cinema. Even in his earliest plays, before he had thought of writing for television or films, he showed a natural tendency to isolate actions and objects from words. What his characters did was often set at a deliberately odd angle in relation to what they said, and physical things – like the dumb waiter in *The Dumb Waiter* – often seem to be invested with a life independent of what the characters do with them. His whole tendency as a writer has been, from the beginning, to bring into close-up objects and gestures which do not normally figure quite so prominently in plays. This is one of the reasons he can adapt his style so readily to media where the camera does the work of bringing the physical detail into focus.

England, unlike America and Italy, has very few writers who devote their whole career to the cinema. Most of our good screenwriters are playwrights – David Mercer, Peter Nichols, Edward Bond, Charles Wood, John Osborne, Robert Bolt, David Storey and John McGrath have produced many of our best post-war screenplays, and what makes Pinter unique even in such distinguished company as this is the strength of his drive towards economy. His technique in his screenplays, as in his stage plays, depends very much on establishing what needs to be established with a minimum of words and using a lot of his dialogue to draw ironical arabesques around the bare bones of his plots. The freedom of movement that cinema provides enables him to construct swiftly in terms of contrasted images, and while, from the beginning, he seemed to find it easier than most playwrights do to resist the temptation of telling the story in terms of words, his self-discipline, his facility for construction, his lightness of touch and his feeling for pattern have helped him to develop a formidable expertise as a screenwriter.

Robin Maugham's novella *The Servant* cannot have been at all easy to adapt as a film, particularly for a writer who then had no experience of the medium. In adapting it to himself for the stage, Robin Maugham had found it impossible to avoid a good deal of clumsy and old-fashioned exposition. Pinter, wisely, ignored Maugham's own dramatization, worked entirely from the original story. Another wise decision was to cut out the character of Richard, the narrator and friend of the hero, Tony. Richard acts as the apostle of reason, trying to restrain Tony from his downward progression into a symbiotic relationship with his servant, Barrett.

Pinter's astringency burns all the sentimental fat and all the superfluous moralizing away from the meat of the story. Its basic idea is a striking one, and the screenplay develops it skilfully, using a maximum of specifics, a minimum of generalization and explanation. Both the story and the play begin with accounts of how Richard found the house for Tony when he was about to return to England from Africa; with his unerring eye for what is relevant, Pinter takes all this for granted. The camera can simply show the house and Tony in possession of it. How he came to be in possession of it is unimportant: what matters is his immaturity and the need this produces for him to have someone to look after him. The film starts with Barrett walking into the house, and we will see, clearly focused, the series of events which enable Barrett virtually to take possession of both the house and its master. Pinter dispenses with all words except the dialogue needed to pinpoint what is happening underneath it. All reference to Tony's experiences in Africa, for instance, is cut.

Tony's relationship with his girl-friend (Sally Grant in the story;

Harold Pinter

Susan Stewart in the film) is realized better by Pinter than by Maugham. Without explaining anything about how they met or Susan's background, Pinter simply introduces a sequence in a night-club where she and Tony are dancing together, both slightly drunk. Then we cut to a scene in the house where they are lying on the still uncarpeted floor of the drawing-room, kissing.

Film is by far the best medium for showing how a house is re-decorated – we can see it happening, and the way in which Barrett takes charge shows how he begins to get his hold on Tony. We also see him waiting on him, providing him with food and drink, making him comfortable – happy to be passive. The close-ups on facial expression which are possible in film also make it easier to be eco-nomical in indicating the beginnings of the antagonism between Susan and Barrett. She will be trying unsuccessfully to pull Tony towards a normal marriage, while Barrett, in the uneven tug-of-war, drags him downwards. Appropriately, the battle begins over the house. Susan's suggestions about decor are effectively undermined by the masterful servant.

By montage, Pinter rapidly makes the essential points both about Barrett and Tony, and about the growing relationship between them.

> Barrett sitting alone on a chair in kitchen, smoking, picking his teeth.
> Exterior. House. Day. Tony running in pouring rain up steps of house.
> Interior. Hall. Day. Tony's wet feet. He takes off his raincoat.
> Interior. Kitchen. Day. Barrett pouring salt into a bowl of warm water.
> Interior. Drawing-room. Day. Tony sitting in library alcove. Barrett undoes his shoes, takes socks off. Tony puts feet in bowl.
>
> TONY: Oh, is this necessary?
> BARRETT: Better to be safe than sorry, sir.
> TONY: You're too skinny to be a nanny, Barrett. (*Barrett looks at him.*) Oh, come on, don't sulk, I didn't mean it. (*He squiggles his feet.*) Oh . . . oh . . . splendid!

In the film, as in the story, Barrett uses a girl to weaken Susan's hold on Tony and to strengthen his own. In the story he pretends that

102

Vera is his niece, in the film, his sister. In both he persuades Tony to
take her on as a housemaid. Pinter's screenplay indicates how the
camera is to show the impact that Vera's body makes on Tony.

> Vera comes in, places tea tray on side table with great care,
> bending over Tony to do so.
> Interior. Drawing-room. Twilight.
> Tony still lying, dozing, a book on the floor, the tea tray empty.
> Vera and Barrett enter with flowers. They arrange the flowers on
> a table by the window. Tony watches through half-open eyes. He
> sees Vera's face and throat through the flowers, her body, in her
> short black maid's uniform, moving under the table, her legs.

Her relationship with Barrett is suggested by a slightly kinky scene
after Tony has caught her using his bathroom. Barrett has told her
to use it, expecting her to be caught, and after Tony goes out,
Barrett announces that he himself is going to have a bath in it. After
Vera has turned the tap on for him he thrusts Tony's bottle of
Cologne into her hands, saying that he wants it all over him.

Her seduction of Tony is accomplished as in the story, during a
contrived absence of Barrett. In Maugham's dramatization Vera
talks to Tony at great length about the sexual desires she feels and
how frustrated they have been, Pinter scarcely lets her talk at all,
making the point about her sexual appetite later, neatly and very
tersely, when Barrett is making love to her in Tony's bed, and she
is comparing Tony's sexual behaviour with Barrett's.

> VERA: Come on . . . oh come on for Christ's sake, put it down.
> BARRETT: I've only had one puff.
> VERA: Oh come on put it down.
> BARRETT: I'm worn out. What's the matter with you?
> VERA: I know someone who wouldn't say no.
> BARRETT: Him? he'd be on the floor.
> (*Bedcreak. Rustle.*)
>   Let me finish this fag. You're like a bloody machine.
> VERA: I know I am but I can't help it.

To enrich the drama of this moment still further, Tony and Susan
are overhearing this conversation.

As in the story, Barrett and Vera are both sacked, but meeting Tony

103

Harold Pinter

in a bar, Barrett persuades him to give him back the job. The trans-
formation of the house that now ensues is demonstrated visually,
without verbal comment.

> Interior. Hall. Tony's house. Day.
> The house is changed. It is airless, dark, oppressive. Curtains and
> blinds are almost constantly drawn. There are no longer any
> flowers. The log fire has been replaced by illuminated gas logs.
> The sleek television in the bedroom has been replaced by a
> heavy Console, now in the drawing-room. Cheap sex magazines
> replace the expensive monthlies. There is an overlay of Barrett
> everywhere. Photos of footballers cellotaped to mirrors. Porno-
> graphic calendars. Nudes stuck in oil paintings. The furniture
> has subtly changed, the rooms no longer possess composition.
> Elegant pornographic books have been yanked from Tony's
> bookshelves and are strewn about. The bookshelves are left
> disordered and heavy with dust. Barrett's brown paper obscene
> books are piled about, and cellophaned piles of photos. The
> ashtrays are crammed full, glasses half empty and empty beer
> bottles are on the liquor trolley. Barrett is now dressed in a
> rough sweater, corduroy trousers and heavy boots.

The games Barrett and Tony now play are entirely Pinter's inven-
tion. The hide-and-seek is extremely effective, with Tony jammed in
a corner of the bathroom, shivering with anticipation, eyes dilated,
as Barrett creeps about looking for him and calling out to him as he
does so. At the climax of the scene Barrett charges into the bathroom
with a maniacal laugh and Tony faints.

Vera, who has not been reinstated in the job, returns to make an
unsuccessful appeal to Tony's mercy. Maugham replaces her with
another girl but Pinter ends the story with an orgy during which
Susan comes to the house.

> BARRETT (to Susan): Do you know where we're going in the
> morning?
> (Pause.)
> We're going to Brazil in the morning. (He grins.) Aren't we
> Tone? (To Susan.) Have a fag.
> Tony lies on the bed staring at Susan. Susan moves to Barrett and
> kisses him. He laughs and holds her. She looks at Tony. His mouth

is open, he moves from the bed. One of the girls touches him. He shivers, stumbles, falls and collapsing, brings tablecloth, glasses, bottles down with him.

The kiss was the director's idea and the film ends without words, using images, movements, sound effects. We see Susan walking away from the house, we see Barrett locking and bolting the front door of the house, we see Tony crawling weakly onto the landing to sit in a corner, we see Barrett climbing up the stairs towards him.

Penelope Mortimer's largely autobiographical novel *The Pumpkin Eater* is a better piece of writing than Maugham's *The Servant*, but more intractable as material for a screenplay, partly because it is such a subjective piece of writing, depending so much on the mood and the tone of voice that the prose suggests, partly because it depends less on its storyline, partly because so much of its significant substance is centred on the central character's relationship with her psychiatrist. While the impact of *The Servant* as a film surpasses that of the original story, the film of *The Pumpkin Eater* does not equal that of the novel, *partly* because of casting and direction, but also partly because Pinter's treatment of the story squeezes out much of the individual flavour that Penelope Mortimer's narrative gave it, without substituting any alternative piquancy, except occasionally in fairly unimportant scenes.

Using facial expression, posture, gesture and lighting to suggest the mood of Jo, the film can easily convey that she is depressed, but cannot convey very much about her depression or its background. It cannot therefore arouse our sympathy for her as the book does, while Pinter's dialogue is more effective in showing her husband's lack of interest in her predicament than in stimulating ours.

The flashes backwards and forwards in time are also very much more confusing and irritating in the film than in the context of discussions with the psychiatrist in the novel. The essential points are clear enough: we gather that before Jo and Jake married they both had several children by previous marriages, and we see his parents trying, kindly, to warn her of the difficulties that may lie ahead. Fairly brief sequences are used to signpost phases in the history of

105

Harold Pinter

their life with their numerous children. We see him trying to write
and being distracted by noise. We see him having an affair with a
younger woman who is living temporarily with them. We see a great
deal of the children in scenes which help to evoke the reality of what
it is generally like to live surrounded by children, but without
specifically throwing light on a woman whose neurosis makes her
want to have more and more of them. Her feelings and especially
her sufferings, which are focused so well in the novel, are eclipsed in
the film by the apparent reasonableness of the man.

> JAKE: Me? You don't care about me. All you care about is that
> bloody great army of children I'm supposed to work my guts
> out for. That's all you care about. Where the hell do I come in?
> (*Pause.*)
> I can't even take a bath in peace, I can't . . . I can't even go to
> bed with you without one of them comes barging in in the
> middle, but so what, you just . . . I'm sick of living in a bloody
> nursery. Where the damn hell do I come in?
> (*She giggles.*)
> What are you sniggering about? It's funny when I tell you
> the truth for once, I suppose.
> JO: The truth?
> JAKE: That I'm capable of fancying someone else. I'm a per-
> fectly normal man who's capable of fancying someone else.

The technique of showing things happening without explanation,
as in *The Servant*, does not work nearly so well with the more tangled
narrative skein of *The Pumpkin Eater*. The sequence in which Jo
starts crying in Harrods is touching but unhelpful: the story is not
one which can be told straightforwardly just through the objective
enactment of specific incidents.

Pinter may have thought of the reduction of the psychiatrist's role
to a very small one in the same terms he thought as of the elimination
of Richard in *The Servant*, but here there is a considerable loss. The
sequences in which she talks to him are curiously unyielding, as if
Pinter were not sympathizing sufficiently with her predicament.

> INGRAM: Tell me about your first husband.
> JO: Oh . . . I can't remember.
> INGRAM: Really? You were married to him for two years.

JO: He was ... sweet ... quite sweet ... Drank a bit, I think
... second one died, he was killed ... he was nice ... third one
was a violinist ... Giles ... he was nice ... we lived in this
barn ... with the children ... hardly went out, really ...
some years, I think ...
INGRAM: Why did you leave him? What happened?
JO: Happened? Nothing happened. Nothing happened at all.

One of the best scenes in the film is one which gains sympathy for
her through a verbal assault on her made by a spiteful woman in a
hairdresser's. Jo is unable to defend herself in any way against the
malice of the woman, who recognizes her from photographs in a
magazine and who, ironically, envies the happiness she thinks Jo
must enjoy, being beautiful and having a wonderful husband and
wonderful children.

Neither the progression of the film towards its climax nor the
climax itself are as well phased as in *The Servant*. After Jo has agreed
to be sterilized and has actually undergone the operation, there is an
effective scene, set at the zoo, in which a friend of theirs, Conway,
tries to make a pass at her and, after failing, reveals that his wife,
Beth, has been having an affair with Jake. Conway's threats are
reminiscent in tone of the conversation of the jealous woman in the
hairdresser's, who finally indicated that she would like to sleep with
Jake and threatened to claw Jo's skin off. Conway's jealousy is
different and his threats of violence are against Jake, but again, the
words are being directed against Jo, and again, Pinter is using the
same device to arouse sympathy for her.

The news that Beth is going to have Jake's baby is also used as a
pretext for a verbal assault on Jo by Conway, this time over the
telephone, and when the two men meet, the dialogue in which
physical violence is sidestepped by ironic verbal violence reminds us
of *The Collection*:

CONWAY: My wife's going to have a baby.
JAKE: Is that so? I say!
CONWAY: Yes, you and your wife must come round to see it. I
understand she's very fond of children.
JAKE: Yes, we'd adore too. How is your wife, by the way?

Harold Pinter

CONWAY: Tip top. She's at a reception tonight for the Duchess of Dubrovnik.

JAKE: I thought she was the Duchess of Dubrovnik.

CONWAY: My wife? No, no, not at all. Not at all. Not at all.

JAKE (*laughing*): Well, you're not the bloody Duke anyway.

(*Jake's glass slips from his hand, falls on Conway's lap and then to the floor. Whisky stains Conway's trousers.*)

CONWAY: You've made me wet.

(*They stare at each other, their faces close together, bending forward on their bar stools.*)

A cemetery scene, in which Jake's father is buried, provides a climactic visual correlative to Jo's sufferings, and then the final sequences of the film take us to the new house in which Jo and Jake, together with the children, are trying to make a fresh start.

Adam Hall's thriller *The Berlin Memorandum* could hardly be more different from *The Pumpkin Eater*. It has a strong story line with espionage, fights, kidnapping, killings, car-chases and all the usual ingredients of cinematic suspense. After idiosyncratically generating his own kind of suspense in his early 'comedies of menace', it is interesting to see Pinter's dialogue and his technique of constructing applied to a more-or-less conventional spy story.

The Quiller Memorandum (as the film is called) begins violently with a man trying to make a call from a telephone box in the Berlin Tiergarten and being shot dead as he dials the second figure. We cut abruptly to a comfortable London club where two British officials are suavely discussing the incident over an enjoyable lunch and selecting a replacement for the man, who has been killed in the same way as his predecessor had been. Cutting back to Berlin, we see Quiller, the replacement, being briefed at the Olympic Stadium by an equally suave, equally British official. The operation, we now learn, is against a group of Neo-Nazis, and we also learn that Kenneth Lindsay Jones, the agent who was killed, might still be alive if he had not refused 'cover' – refused to let other agents follow him around. Later, of course, we will see Quiller taking the same risk.

Hengel, the agent who will be covering him, first of all hands over an envelope containing clues – two torn tickets, one from a bowling alley, one from a swimming-pool, and a newspaper cutting with the headline 'School Teacher Arrested – War Crimes'. Both the bowling alley and the swimming-pool provide visually lively locales for the two scenes which follow, as Quiller starts his investigations, and the love interest starts when, pretending to be a journalist, he goes to the school at which the teacher who was arrested as a war criminal had been working. The headmistress, who speaks little English, introduces him to a beautiful young teacher who speaks more. Thrillers no longer have to explain everything neatly in the way that they used to, and Pinter's treatment of Inge Lindt leaves a great deal unexplained. Though she is obviously attracted to Quiller, there are indications that she knows more than she is willing to tell him about the ex-war-criminal and a conversation about Joe Louis and a German boxer, Schmeling, makes it seem that she may be sceptical about whether 'the old Germany' has finally been defeated.

It is immediately after the scene with Inge, in which he reveals his interest in the Neo-Nazis, that they appear to have become aware of his presence in Berlin. He finds a man is following him in the street, and soon afterwards, apparently accidentally, a hotel porter bumps into him while carrying a suitcase which hits against his leg. Driving his hired car he finds himself overcome with fatigue: the sharp edge of the suitcase has injected him with a drug. A Mercedes draws up beside his car as he stops at a traffic light and he is driven to the enemy's base.

The interrogation, conducted by a man who calls himself Oktober, is peppered with questions and evasions which are reminiscent of the interrogation in *The Birthday Party*.

QUILLER: Listen, can I make a suggestion?
OKTOBER: Surely. But we would like to know your name first.
QUILLER: Let me make this suggestion first.
OKTOBER: No. Tell us your name first.
(*Pause.*)
QUILLER: They call me Spike.
OKTOBER: Not your nickname. Your surname.
QUILLER: Canetti.
(*Pause.*)
OKTOBER: What is your suggestion?

QUILLER: I think this is a case of mistaken identity. I work for
  Doubledays in New York. I came to Berlin looking for rare
  books.
OKTOBER: Have you found them?
QUILLER: Well no, not quite yet. I haven't found them yet.
  (*Oktober smiles.*)
OKTOBER: What is your real name?
QUILLER: My mother's maiden name was O'Reilly.
OKTOBER: What is your real name, please, Mr Quiller?
QUILLER: Well, originally I had to walk around with a double-
  barrelled name. O'Reilly Canetti. But I found it a bit heavy
  (*Turns to Doctor.*) Wouldn't you find it heavy? So I dropped
  the O'Reilly and kept the Canetti.
OKTOBER: What does your father do, Mr Quiller?
QUILLER: He's dead.
OKTOBER: And your mother?
QUILLER: She's dead too.
OKTOBER: And your sister?
QUILLER: She's dead too. What I mean is I never had one. I
  was an only child.
OKTOBER: You must be lonely.
QUILLER: No, no, . . . no.
OKTOBER: You must feel lonely now, sitting here amongst
  strangers.
QUILLER: No, I like meeting people. You know . . . new
  faces . . .

As in the television play *Tea Party*, tricks of vision are recreated
through visual tricks. When Quiller, who has been injected hypo-
dermically with a drug, escapes into a doze, he is jerked back into
consciousness with another injection, and we see the room as he
does, in abnormally sharp focus, while the ticking of a watch is
preternaturally sharp. Of course he resists heroically the drug they
have administered to make him talk, and the sequence ends as
Oktober instructs the doctor to inject him and the guards to kill him
when he's unconscious.

Again we cut to the London club. At a well-equipped bar the same
two men cheerfully discuss the Berlin situation in the same breath
as the Lord Mayor's Banquet, to which one of them, already in full
evening dress, is going. Cutting back to Berlin we see Quiller's body

at the edge of a river, but he is not dead. Surprised to be alive, he hauls himself to his feet, staggers to a bar, finds a hotel and telephones Inge, who agrees to see him tomorrow. Summoned to meet his superiors, Quiller still insists on operating without cover, and promises to find the enemy base to which he was taken, but refuses to say how.

When Inge, to whom he now describes himself as 'a kind of investigator', offers to introduce him to a friend of her father's who used to be one of 'them', we are taken back to the swimming-pool, now empty. Their figures are shown dramatically in long shot at the far corner of the pool, and their voices echo ominously. The friend, who is the attendant of the pool, offers to introduce Quiller to Schroeder, who turns out to be the headmistress we have already met. She points out the house. Leaving Inge in the car as the others leave, Quiller gives her a telephone number to ring if he is not back within twenty minutes. There is a suspenseful sequence as he breaks into the house. At first it seems to be empty; then he sees several men who appear to be waiting for him. They bring him to Oktober. When he is taken down to the cellar, Inge is there. He pretends not to know her, but, undeceived, they offer to let him go free, threatening to kill her unless he divulges the whereabouts of the English base before dawn.

What follows is a tense late-night sequence in which he is followed through the streets and into bars by members of the group, who would interfere if he tried to telephone his superiors. Eventually he eludes them at an overhead railway station by jumping on a train just as it is leaving. Returning to his hotel, he finds a bomb attached to the underside of his car. After staging an explosion to make them think he has been killed, he gives his superiors the address of the Nazi base, but in the successful raid they make on it no girl is found.

When Quiller meets Inge to say good-bye, she tells him that they let her go. The film ends without resolving the enigma: he asks her whether she ever knew a man called Jones and she denies it.

The screenplay for *Accident* is a more ambitious piece of writing, and the resulting film is the best Pinter had written since *The Servant*.

111

Harold Pinter

Nicholas Mosley's novel is a less straightforward piece of narrative than Robin Maugham's long story, but it lends itself well to objectification in terms of the cut-and-dried, cut-and-thrust technique Pinter had been developing as a screenwriter. Like the novel, the film begins with the accident in which William, the student, is killed. The novel is narrated by Stephen, the don; the film follows suit at least in having scarcely any action (once the accident itself is over) in which he does not figure.

The screenplay is like that of *The Quiller Memorandum* in starting with abrupt violence, a frightening montage of shots, in some of which she seems to be standing on his chest or his head, and moving to a more restful key, but here there is no abrupt transition. We modulate into the aftermath of the accident: Stephen with Anna in his house, the police arriving and then (in a scene without Anna but with no explanation of where she has disappeared) they are asking questions, suggesting that William was drunk because of the amount of whisky in the car. We then see Anna settled upstairs in a four-poster bed. She is asleep and Stephen is watching her. After a brief flashback to the accident – her shoe digging into William's dead face while Stephen's voice shouts 'Don't' – we are moved right back into the past when William was alive, at Oxford, talking to Stephen, who is tutor to both of them, about Anna, an Austrian princess.

All the sequences in the early part of the film are brief. Soon we cut to Stephen's family life. He has a son of seven, a daughter of three, and his wife, Rosalind, is pregnant again. In a short scene in the dons' Common Room at the college we meet Charley Hall, who is talking about sex, the Provost and a scientist called Hedges, but as the Provost begins to tell a story, we cut away to a punting scene with William, Anna and Stephen. We do not see Stephen fall into the river but we see him walking back with William, soaking wet to his rooms, blaming himself bad-temperedly for growing old and losing his judgment of distance.

Stephen invites William and Anna to his house for Sunday lunch. Charley, one of whose books Stephen has loaned to Anna, arrives, uninvited, and stays. He writes novels, and a conversation about novels, for which he says all you need is a starting point, leads him

112

on to take that moment, on the lawn, as a possible starting point, asking what they are all up to:

CHARLEY: Describe what we're all doing.
(*William looks about the garden.*)
WILLIAM: Rosalind's lying down. Stephen's weeding the garden. Anna's making a daisy chain. We're having this conversation.
CHARLEY: Good. But then you could go further. Rosalind is pregnant. Stephen's having an affair with a girl at Oxford. He's reached the age when he can't keep his hands off girls at Oxford.
WILLIAM: What?
CHARLEY: But he feels guilty, of course. So he makes up a story.
WILLIAM: What story?
CHARLEY: This story.
WILLIAM: What are you talking about?
(*Charley sits up, swats violently at flies.*)
CHARLEY: Oh, these flies are terrible.
WILLIAM: What flies? There aren't any flies.
CHARLEY: They're Sicilian horse flies, from Corsica.
(*Charlie shouts across lawn.*)
    Have you heard our conversation?
(*Stephen weeding.*)
STEPHEN: Yes!
(*Rosalind lying, eyes closed.*)
ROSALIND: Yes.

From this scene, which is sharp in the novel and still sharper in the film, we cut tellingly to the first game – tennis. Charley is playing barefoot, with Anna as his partner, against William and Stephen. Charley's service hits Anna in the back. Stephen serves into the net. Anna, hitting wildly, knocks the ball into the bushes. Charley's service again hits Anna. William's powerful service beats Charley, who falls flat on his back. Almost like the Dumb Show in Hamlet, the game has silently prefigured much of what is to follow.

Afterwards Anna refuses to go for a walk with William but volunteers to go for one with Stephen. There seems to be a moment, when they pause at a stile, when he could touch her if he dared to. His hand stays close to hers on top of the stile and then it is too late. She is suggesting they go back.

113

Harold Pinter

A drunken after-dinner conversation reveals that Charley appears regularly on television, and Stephen, who seems to be envious of this, says that he has an appointment to meet Charley's producer in London.

When Stephen, who has been dozing drunkenly in a kitchen chair, finally goes up to bed, he sees a woman in a negligee with frilled cuffs at the top of the stairs. Going into his bedroom he has the illusion that the woman in the four-poster is Anna, and he calls her by name, but it is his wife. He tells her that he loves her.

Stephen's visit to the offices of the television company is unsuccessful. The producer is ill and the man who has taken over the programme shows very little interest in having Stephen on it. He consoles himself by visiting an ex-girl-friend, the Provost's daughter, Francesca. There is no synchronized dialogue in the scene with her.

> The only sounds heard are the voices overlaid at stated points. The words are fragments of realistic conversation. They are not thoughts. Nor are they combined with any lip movement on the part of the actors. They are distributed over the sequence so as to act as a disembodied comment on the action.

Returning to his house, which ought to be empty because Rosalind is away, Stephen is disconcerted to find Charley has been sleeping there with Anna. There is also a letter from Charley's wife telling Stephen about the affair: Charley opens it and reads it to him. Masochistically, Stephen questions Charley about when the affair started and stops Anna even from making the bed they have used.

The next game is played at an aristocratic country house where Stephen and William are both guests. It is a viciously aggressive variant of the Eton wall game with a heavy cushion as the ball. The script describes the scrum as 'a communal buggery' and there is undisguised kicking, butting and elbowing in the stomach. Stephen, who is in goal, savagely knees William in the face before being felled himself by a blow from behind.

We cut straight to a game of cricket – William hitting savagely at a ball to the sound of applause. Returning to the pavilion when he has been caught out, William tells Stephen that he is going to marry Anna. Asked by Anna to tell Charley, Stephen invites them both to

his house. Flashes of the accident sequence tell us that this invitation led to the fatal journey. We then flash forward to the scene after the accident, when Stephen has Anna alone in his house and takes advantage of her, using his knowledge that she was driving the car when it crashed, though the police do not know that anyone but William was in the car. (In the novel, Stephen's desire for her remains unsatisfied.) Afterwards he helps her to climb over the wall into her college, and in the final scene with Charley, who cannot understand Anna's decision to go back home, Stephen is for once at an advantage. Charley had not even been told of the engagement between Anna and William.

The Go-Between is a less successful adaptation and again the basic reason can be found in the intractability of the novel. It is a good novel, but though the bulk of the action, wedged between a prologue and an epilogue, is set in 1900, the book, which was published in 1953, belongs very much to that period. Much of the fiction written in England during the ten years after the war was devoted to evocations of childhood, and in *The Go-Between* we are asked to believe that a man's life could be ruined by premature exposure to the rough reality of sexual relationships. The central character, presented in the prologue and epilogue as a desiccated old man who has never fully lived, remembers a childhood country holiday during which an upper-class girl and a farmer who were having an affair used him to take messages to arrange their meetings. The final revelation of the animal ugliness of the act of love between adults who had each seemed too glamorous is a traumatic experience from which the boy never fully recovers.

In the seventies it is much harder than it was in the fifties to believe in the book's basic premiss. To accept the extent of the psychological damage the shock could do, it is necessary to recreate in our much more permissive moral climate not only the mores of 1900 but the mores of the early fifties, and while Pinter's screenplay succeeds reasonably well with the turn of the century, it tries to sidestep what is really the central problem of adaptation by saying:

> The 'present' is any time in the last 20 years.

Harold Pinter

Dispensing with the simple sandwiching of the main narrative between a prologue and an epilogue set in the present tense, Pinter bases his screenplay on the epilogue, which deals with the narrator's visit to the old woman who was once in love with the farmer, and from this he shuttles backwards and forwards into the past. As in *Accident*, he makes good use of the novel's dialogue, selecting well and sharpening points by pruning. The dialogue between Leo – the narrator as schoolboy – and Marcus – the friend who has invited him for a summer holiday at his family's house – is charming.

> Interior. Bedroom.
> Marcus is in bed. The dog growls.
>
> LEO: What's up?
> MARCUS: Decent of you to trickle along, but don't come in. I have a headache and some spots. Mama thinks it may be measles.
> LEO: Hard cheese.
> MARCUS: See Trimingham?
> LEO: Is he the man with the face?
> MARCUS: Yes. Got it in the war. He was gored by the Boers.
> LEO: Hard cheese.

It is Marcus's confinement in bed which leaves Leo isolated and exposes him to the danger of exploitation by the charming but selfish lovers. It is the farmer, Ted Burgess, who gives him the first message, and Marian, Marcus's sister, is quick to realize how useful it would be to have a messenger whom no one would suspect. The actual message-carrying, with its half-guilty hurrying journeys through lush summer countryside between Brandham Hall and the farm, naturally provides rich food for the camera, and Pinter's screenplay is full of cues which were cleverly taken by Joseph Losey, the director, who made good use of the Norfolk locations. The beauty of the scenery was one of the film's best features.

But this is only one of the reasons that (except in the scenes between the schoolboys) the actual words the characters are given to speak make less impact than usual in a Pinter film. Neither Marian nor Ted are characterized very strongly in terms of dialogue. Hartley's novel presents them through the schoolboy's flattering vision.

The Screenplays

The camera is more objective. It can linger on the attractive faces and physiques of Julie Christie and Alan Bates, but as characters they still emerge less memorably than the unfortunate Lord Trimingham, the man Marian at first rejects, though later she accepts his offer of marriage, because she is pregnant. Trimingham, particularly in his scenes alone with Leo, is endowed with an endearing mixture of conventionality, humour, self-irony and the capacity for side-stepping questions which is characteristic of Pinter's characters.

TRIMINGHAM: Sit down. Cigar?

LEO: No thank you.

(*Trimingham sits down and lights a cigar.*)
   Can I ask you something?

TRIMINGHAM: You can.

LEO: I was reading a book. And in this book . . . two men fought a duel . . . over a quarrel . . . about one of the men's wife. And then . . . in this duel . . . the wife's husband . . . the husband . . . was shot.

TRIMINGHAM: Mmn-hmnm. (*Pause.*) What's your question?

LEO: Well, I thought . . . when I read it . . . that it was prob-ably the lady's fault, but she didn't have to fight the duel and I just thought that it was a little unfair.

(*Close-up of Trimingham.*)

TRIMINGHAM: Nothing is ever a lady's fault.

(*Close-up of Leo.*)

LEO: Oh.

(*Close-up of Trimingham.*)

TRIMINGHAM: Does that answer your question?

(*Shot across Trimingham to Leo.*)

LEO: Yes.

TRIMINGHAM: Any other questions?

LEO: Er . . . what do you think of Ted Burgess?

TRIMINGHAM (*ruminatively*): What do I think of Ted Burgess?
   (*Pause.*) He's a powerful hitter.

(*Leo chuckles.*)
   But you had the measure of him.

(*Leo smiles.*)
   You defeated him, didn't you? (*Pause.*) Yes, Ted Burgess is quite a decent fellow. A bit wild.

LEO: Wild? Do you mean he's dangerous?

Harold Pinter

TRIMINGHAM: He's not dangerous to you or me. He's a bit of a lady-killer, that's all.

LEO (*baffled*): A lady-killer?

The description of Ted as a 'powerful hitter' and the adult compliment to Leo for having the measure of him refer to a game of cricket in which Leo finally caught him out.

Again the game is used to prefigure the action that is to ensue. Leo will involuntarily be the means by which Ted's relationship with Marian is discovered. Mrs Maudsley discovers him in possession of a love letter and (with a heavy rainstorm as the slightly melodramatic background for the incident) forces Leo to lead her to the outhouse, shrouded symbolically in deadly nightshade, where Ted and Marian are making love and just approaching a climax as they are discovered. Ted later commits suicide.

Past and present are closely interwoven in the final sequences of the film and Pinter manfully struggles with his intractable material, trying to streamline an old-fashioned climax by approximating to the style of his recent plays which focus on the tricks memory plays in recreating past relationships. But of course a mere visual juxtaposition between a dramatization of past events and shots of the old man that Leo grows into does not suffice to clarify the relationship between them.

CONCLUSION

Reading Konrad Lorenz's book *On Aggression,* I was struck again and again by the similarities between the animal behaviour he describes and the behaviour of Pinter's characters. There are so many battles for territory and battles for possession of the female. Lorenz tells us how an aquarium six feet long wasn't big enough for two young coral fish, scarcely an inch long. One had to live in a corner behind the bubbles of an air-generator while the other patrolled the rest of the space. The main reason coral fish are coloured so brightly is that this has the effect of making them fight fish who wear the same colours – not fighting to the death, but driving the rivals away so that they don't compete for the same food in the same water. The animal's readiness to fight depends partly on the distance he is from the centre of the territory he 'owns'. Often, when one animal is chasing another away from its home territory, the fugitive, arriving on home ground, turns to attack the pursuer vigorously and unexpectedly, driving him away and pursuing, and the process repeats itself until the combatants achieve a point of balance where they threaten each other without fighting. Julian Huxley has compared animal territories with air balloons pressing against each other in a glass container and expanding or contracting in accordance with the variations in internal pressure.

Most animals become vicious and more territorially greedy when they have paired but, looking at *The Homecoming* in these terms, Teddy has the disadvantage of being away from what is now his home and coming into the lair of a particularly aggressive family who mob together against him, as they have against Sam.

It is no accident that the motif of hunting occurs so often in Pinter's work, as it does in Beckett's. The motives for the pursuit may often remain obscure but the panic of the quarry and the excitement of the chase are shown in animal terms. The hunt in *The Dumb Waiter* has all the more suspense for the fact that the two hunters themselves feel puzzled and hunted, afraid of what is going on outside the room. Stanley, in *The Birthday Party,* is terrified when he hears that two strangers are coming to the boarding-house and the hunt is translated into nightmare terms both in the game of blindman's-buff and when the lights go out. The nightmare sequence of hunting in the dark is repeated in Pinter's screenplay for *The Servant* in the game of hide-and-seek. The master becomes like a guilty child when the adults scare him by telling him that the Bogy Man is coming for him. There are variations on the terror in the dark and on the panicky feeling that someone is after you, in Mick's pursuit of Davies with a vacuum cleaner and in Disson's trouble with his eyes in *Tea Party,* which makes him all the more confused about the way Willy and the two women are combining to persecute him. Edward's eye trouble in *A Slight Ache* seems to hide the feeling of being threatened in some way by the matchseller, and in *A Night Out,* Gidney has had it in for Albert partly because he let the side down in the football match and partly because he is different from the others, immature, a mother's boy, quiet, not one for the girls. And in Albert, as in all the other characters, the combination of guilt with a feeling of personal inadequacy heightens the feeling of persecution. Often we get the impression of a pack of animals closing in on their prey, particularly as the girls join in the game of teasing Albert in the party scene and in *The Homecoming* when the family gang up against Teddy.

Pinter's own position, as an observer, outside things, is not unlike that of the naturalist, inspecting humanity through the glass wall of the aquarium tank. In a lecture he gave at the *Sunday Times* Student Drama Festival in 1962, he said:

> There are two silences. One when no word is spoken. The other when perhaps a torrent of language is being employed. This speech is speaking of a language locked beneath it. That is its continual reference. The speech we hear is an indication of that we don't hear. It is a necessary avoidance, a violent, sly, anguished or mocking smokescreen which keeps the other in its place. When true silence falls we are still left with echo but are nearer nakedness. One way of looking at speech is to say it is a constant stratagem to cover nakedness.

One way of looking at Pinter's work is to say that it is a constant stratagem to uncover nakedness. The behaviour of his characters is so seldom a reflection of the way people normally behave and so often a reflection of the way they would like to, if they weren't afraid to, or a refraction of fears and anxieties in the form of actions. Violence occurs because animality is unleashed and, unlike the Greeks who took a high view of human dignity and kept the violence off-stage, Pinter peers in through the glass wall with no reverence for humanity, no belief in our lives being mapped out by divine powers and a keen eye for the cracks in the surface of normal conversation and normal behaviour. He is always on the alert for the moments when his characters betray what is underneath and then he simply records what he sees and what he hears, not in order to evolve theories and not in order to warn us against ourselves. His vision and his hearing are both highly tuned instruments, invaluable in his one-man forays into the unarticulated and irrational no-man's-land inside the modern Everyman.

He is often accused of repeating himself, but, in his kind of play, I don't think the charge is a damaging one except where the repetition is more of manner than of matter. In *The Homecoming* and in *Tea Party* he was probably relying too much on the tricks he had learned for hypnotizing an audience into rapt attentiveness. In the screen-play for *Accident* and in *Tea Party*, he manages to go over familiar territory with unfamiliar visual images and a new speed (again visual) in tacking from one set of images to the next. In *Landscape*, *Silence* and *Night* he is breaking into new ground and writing more poetically than ever before. But *Old Times* does not continue the tendency.

He once said that he dealt with his characters 'at the extreme edge of their living.' The later plays rely less on violence to push them into that position, but the best of them allow the characters more freedom for the violence to well up inside once they are there. While the impulses and ideas that he welcomes over the threshold of inarticulacy are still disturbing, *Old Times* is more teasing than frightening, more stylish than stylistically experimental. Success seems to have brought a security which has stilled the neurotic urgency that made the early plays so electrifying. Their triumph was to find theatrical effects that were exactly ·coefficient to the febrile pulsing of an inexpressible terror. The mature Pinter has mastered the demons that once possessed him. He is still a master of theatrical effects, but now they are created mainly because they are effective.